DINNER WITH LENNY

DINNER

with

LENNY

THE LAST LONG INTERVIEW WITH
LEONARD BERNSTEIN

Jonathan Cott

OXFORD
UNIVERSITY PRESS

OXFORD

UNIVERSITY PRESS

Oxford University Press is a department of the
University of Oxford. It furthers the University's objective
of excellence in research, scholarship, and education
by publishing worldwide.

Oxford   New York
Auckland   Cape Town   Dar es Salaam   Hong Kong   Karachi
Kuala Lumpur   Madrid   Melbourne   Mexico City   Nairobi
New Delhi   Shanghai   Taipei   Toronto

With offices in
Argentina   Austria   Brazil   Chile   Czech Republic   France   Greece
Guatemala   Hungary   Italy   Japan   Poland   Portugal   Singapore
South Korea   Switzerland   Thailand   Turkey   Ukraine   Vietnam

Oxford is a registered trademark of Oxford University Press
in the UK and certain other countries.

Published in the United States of America by
Oxford University Press
198 Madison Avenue, New York, NY 10016

Library of Congress Cataloging-in-Publication Data
Cott, Jonathan.
Dinner with Lenny : the last long interview
with Leonard Bernstein / Jonathan Cott.
p. cm.
Includes bibliographical references and index.
ISBN 978-0-19-985844-6
1. Bernstein, Leonard, 1918–1990—Interviews.
2. Musicians—United States—Interviews.   I. Title.
ML410.B566C68 2013   780.92—dc23
[B] 2012008756

1 3 5 7 9 8 6 4 2

Printed in the United States of America
on acid-free paper

The temple bell stops—
but the sound keeps coming
out of the flowers.

BASHŌ

(Trans. by Robert Bly)

CONTENTS

DINNER WITH LENNY

PRELUDE

"WOW!" A GALVANIZED Igor Stravinsky reportedly exclaimed after listening to Leonard Bernstein's astonishing recording of *The Rite of Spring*—a still-unsurpassed performance that Columbia Records captured more than fifty years ago in a single inspired and electrically charged recording session on January 20, 1958, in New York City.

In 1791 in the city of Bologna, the Italian physician Luigi Galvani (from whom the word "galvanize" takes its name) demonstrated the electrical basis of nerve impulses when he caused the muscles of dead frogs' legs to twitch by jolting them with a spark from an electrostatic machine. Today, we might look upon Stravinsky's

The Rite of Spring as the musical equivalent of Galvani's machine. This high-voltage sound stimulator—a work that Leonard Bernstein has characterized as "only one of your everyday volcanic masterpieces...a miraculous new creation of such originality and power that still today it shocks and overwhelms us"—in fact provoked a riot at its infamous Paris premiere a century ago in 1913. The well-heeled opening night audience greeted the late-May performance with an outbreak of fashionably partisan booing, whistling, hissing, and catcalling, which rapidly segued into scuffles, fistfights in the aisles, and then with people hitting each other with canes and barking like dogs—culminating in a half-hearted intervention on the part of the Paris police. In the words of Harvard professor Thomas Kelly: "The pagans on-stage made pagans of the audience."

Igor Stravinsky once spoke of the "violent Russian spring" that he vividly recalled from his childhood, and which, he said, seemed "to begin in an hour and was like the whole earth cracking." In a television lecture entitled "Homage to Stravinsky" that he gave at a London Symphony concert in 1972, Bernstein observed that the composer was "born in the spring and died in the spring. In a sense, he lived his whole life in a springtime of creativity. All his music is springlike, newly budding, rooted in the familiar past, yet fresh and sharp, with that stinging, paradoxical combination of the inevitable and the unexpected." And in his incandescent recorded enactment of Stravinsky's pagan vernal rite, Bernstein, leading a galvanized New York Philharmonic, glories in and exploits this revolutionary work's jagged rhythms, rebarbative dissonances, fragmented meters, off-kilter accents, and agitated mood-swinging dynamics in order to communicate the miraculous birthing of that Russian spring.

———————

BORN ON AUGUST 25, 1918, in Lawrence, Massachusetts, Leonard Bernstein was the son of Ukrainian Jewish parents; his father, Sam, ran a successful hair and beauty salon business in Boston. A musically precocious child, Bernstein was educated at the Boston Latin School, Harvard University, the Curtis Institute of Music, and the Tanglewood Summer School. After completing his studies, he moved in the fall of 1942 to New York City where he rented a one-room basement apartment for eight dollars a week and took odd jobs as a music transcriber and as a rehearsal pianist accompanying dance classes at one of the studios in

Carnegie Hall. The choreographer Agnes de Mille recalls that when Bernstein felt bored playing in the invariable meter required by the dance class, he would occasionally slip in a bar of 5/8 or 7/8—and he was once fired for such insubordination.

Aaron Copland, whom Bernstein had met when he was in his junior year at Harvard and who would become a lifelong friend and mentor, wrote him encouraging letters. "Don't expect miracles," Copland advised the young man, "and don't get depressed if nothing happens for a while. That's NY." But on August 25, 1943, his twenty-fifth birthday, Bernstein got his first professional break when Artur Rodzinski, then the music director of the New York Philharmonic, chose him to become his conducting assistant. "I have gone through all the conductors I know of in my mind," Rodzinski explained to his new assistant, "and I finally asked God whom I should take, and God said, 'Take Bernstein.'"

Three months later, the Almighty interceded once again, providing his Chosen One with the ultimate life-changing opportunity: Bernstein would make his legendary conductorial debut with the New York Philharmonic, substituting for an ailing Bruno Walter on only a few hours' notice at a Sunday afternoon Carnegie Hall concert on November 14, 1943.

PRELUDE

Bernstein had been out partying that Saturday night, playing boogie-woogie piano and, as he put it, "carrying on like mad" at a post-concert reception for the opera singer Jennie Tourel, whom he had accompanied earlier that evening at her New York debut recital at Town Hall. Featured on her program was the New York premiere of Bernstein's *I Hate Music! A Cycle of Five Kid Songs* for soprano and piano, which one reviewer praised as "witty, alive, and adroitly fashioned." Sometime between four o'clock and dawn, Bernstein returned home with a hangover. At nine in the morning, he was awakened by a phone call from the Philharmonic's associate manager who told him, "Well, this is it. You have to conduct at three o'clock. No chance of a rehearsal. You will report at a quarter of three backstage."

Bernstein's father, Sam, his mother, Jennie, and his twelve-year-old brother, Burton, had traveled down from Massachusetts to attend the Tourel recital, and were supposed to return home on Sunday afternoon. Bernstein immediately telephoned his father and mother to tell them to postpone their travel plans because Bruno Walter was sick with the flu and that he was going to be replacing him for the Philharmonic's nationally broadcast matinée performance. And that they should wish him good luck. *Oy gevalt!* was his parents' reaction.

A bleary-eyed Bernstein went down to the Carnegie Pharmacy across the street from Carnegie Hall for his customary morning coffee. The druggist, who knew him, said, "You look terrible—what's the matter?" Bernstein told him he had to conduct that afternoon, so, like Lewis Carroll's White Rabbit, the druggist gave him two pills— a phenobarbital and a Benzedrine—and instructed him: "One will calm you down, the other will give you energy." Years later, in the 1978 documentary film *Reflections*, directed by Peter Rosen, Bernstein recalled that legendary performance: "So there I am standing in the wings. All atremble with these two little pills in my pocket....And I took them out and looked at them and said, 'I'm going to do this on my own. I am not going to take any pills. I don't want any aid from anybody but God,' and I just flung them across the entire backstage and strode out, and that's the last thing I remember until the end of the concert when I saw the entire audience there, standing and cheering and screaming. But from the time of my entrance until the time of my last exit I remember nothing. There's nothing I can tell you. It was all a dream."

As Jacques Margolies, one of the Philharmonic violinists who was playing that afternoon, told Bernstein's biographer Meryle Secrest: "We were there a few minutes early. I was young, but that orchestra was really seasoned. The idea was that Bernstein would follow us, only it didn't work out that way. You just couldn't believe a young man could create that kind of music. Here were players in their fifties and sixties with long experience. And here this little snot-nose comes in and creates a more exciting performance. We were supposed to have gone over it with Bruno Walter, we had rehearsed it with him and performed it with him, but this had nothing to do with Bruno Walter. The orchestra stood up and cheered. We were open-mouthed. That man was the most extraordinary musician I have met in my life."[1]

The first work on that historic debut program was Schumann's *Manfred* Overture, based on the poem by Lord Byron. And indeed Leonard Bernstein truly led a life of Byronic intensity—passionate, polyamorous, risk-taking, convention-breaking, continually productive, universally inspiring. From the start, he conducted with a flamboyance and obvious rapture that led some critics to accuse the young maestro of being exhibitionistic and overemotional on the podium. But as Bernstein once asserted: "Life without music is unthinkable. Music without life is academic. That is why my contact with music is a total embrace"—echoing the cry in Schiller's

"Ode to Joy," *Seid umschlugen, Millionen!* ("You millions, I embrace you!").

Unlike almost any other classical performer of recent times, Leonard Bernstein adamantly, and sometimes controversially, refused to compartmentalize and separate his emotional, intellectual, political, erotic, and spiritual longings from the musical experience, describing it in his 1973 Charles Eliot Norton lectures at Harvard University as a "marriage of form and passion" with its occasional "bliss of ambiguities." (When considering whether he should or should not conduct Mahler's reconstituted Tenth Symphony, he unabashedly said to a colleague, "I have one question. Will it give me an orgasm?") And when, in his 1967 essay "Mahler: His Time Has Come," Bernstein defines what he saw as the "dualistic energy source" of the composer's symphonies—with which he always had an extraordinary affinity—he might very well have been suggesting a sense of his own complex, multifaceted musical and personal self, as when he describes Mahler as "rough-hewn *and* epicene, subtle *and* blatant, refined, raw, objective, maudlin, brash, shy, grandiose, self-annihilating, confident, insecure, adjective, opposite, adjective, opposite."[2]

Above all, in every aspect of his life and work, Bernstein was a boundless enthusiast. In the course of my dinner conversation with him, he informed me that the word "enthusiasm" was derived from the Greek adjective *entheos*, meaning "having the god within," with its attendant sense of "living without aging," as did the gods on Mount Olympus. One of my favorite Bernstein stories that perfectly exemplifies and highlights his enthusiastic disposition tells of the occasion when the conductor invited the then twenty-eight-year-old Michael Jackson—another age-defying musical "god" whom Bernstein wildly admired—to attend a concert he was leading with the New York Philharmonic in 1986 at Los Angeles's Royce Hall. Jackson was bowled over by Bernstein's hyperkinetic performance, and during the intermission he went backstage to pay tribute to his fellow musical potentate. The hyper-appreciative Bernstein then wrapped both his arms around Jackson, lifted him up and kissed him on the lips. Landing back on terra firma, the breathless singer found himself only able to ask the conductor, "Do you always use the same baton?" And in 1973, when Bernstein was invited to Rome to conduct a papal concert in the presence of a different category of potentate, Pope Paul VI, a friend cabled him before the concert with a warning: "REMEMBER: THE RING NOT THE LIPS!"

Although, like a Greek god, Leonard Bernstein remained forever young, he had little time and patience for shamming, standing on ceremony, or social masking. He refused to put on supercilious or elitist airs; relished and displayed a disarming frankness and a thoroughly blatant sense of humor; and insistently and fearlessly spoke out against any manner of social and political hypocrisy, making himself a target for occasional reproof and ridicule.

Following his triumphant debut with the New York Philharmonic in 1943, and having overnight attained the status of "boy-wonder"—as well as being lionized by the press on what almost seemed like a daily basis—he received a letter of admonition from his mother, Jennie: "Lenny dear," she wrote, "please don't tell reporters of your personal views...it's very bad taste. It will not do you much good. It may have bad repercussions. From now on you should be very conservative in your statements to the public. Just a little advice from your mother and I'm sure it will not harm you."

Bernstein did not heed his mother's advice; and it is unsettling to discover that during the reign of J. Edgar Hoover, the Federal Bureau of Investigation kept an active file of almost seven hundred pages on Bernstein's political opinions and activities from as early as the mid-1940s. In his book *Leonard Bernstein: The Political Life of an American Musician*, Barry Seldes reveals that Bernstein was blacklisted from 1950 to 1954 and had his passport renewal application rejected by the U.S. State Department in 1953 due to suspected Communist ties (although Bernstein had never been a member of the Communist Party).[3] Then, several months before the September 8, 1971, premiere of Bernstein's *Mass*—a music-theater extravaganza blending pop music and the Catholic liturgy that was written at the request of Jacqueline Kennedy Onassis for the inauguration of the Kennedy Center for the Performing Arts—the FBI warned the Nixon White House that Bernstein might potentially be mounting a plot to "embarrass the President and other Government officials." This led Nixon and his chief of staff H. R. Haldeman to worry that subversive messages might possibly be encoded in some of the work's Latin texts. The president declined to attend the premiere, but Bernstein nevertheless received Nixon's highest accolade when, on the Watergate Tapes, the president is heard calling the composer a "son of a bitch."

In other circles, however, Leonard Bernstein was one of the most honored creative artists of the twentieth century, and certainly one of the most productive. The recipient of twenty-three Grammy Awards, ten Emmy Awards, and twenty-two honorary degrees, he was also the author of five books, of which *The Joy of Music* (1960) and *The Infinite Variety of Music* (1966) still remain two of the most popular and illuminating guides to classical music.

Most famously, he was the conductor of fifty-three legendary Young People's Concerts and of four hundred-plus audio, and dozens of video, recordings—the largest discography of any classical artist—and the composer of exceptional compositions in many genres, including the musicals *West Side Story* and *On the Town*; the operetta *Candide*; the opera *A Quiet Place*; the ballet *Fancy Free*; the soundtrack to the film *On the Waterfront*; the *Jeremiah*, *The Age of Anxiety*, and *Kaddish* symphonies; the choral work *Chichester Psalms*; and the controversial *Mass: A Theater Piece for Singers, Players, and Dancers* ... as well as my, perhaps odd, personal favorite of his works, the *Prelude, Fugue and Riffs* for solo clarinet and jazz ensemble. Composed in 1949 for Woody Herman's big band, and lasting barely nine minutes, this piece of inspired musical *jouissance*—a showcase for the Bernsteinian esthetic of joy—transports the listener into the scintillating sound-worlds of Stravinsky's *Ebony Concerto*, Count Basie's "Riff Interlude," Lionel

Hampton's "Flying Home," and Kurt Weill's *Liebeslied* from *The Threepenny Opera*. One of my most cherished Bernstein moments occurs on the DVD performance of *Prelude, Fugue and Riffs* where we see him transforming members of the Vienna Philharmonic into a truly credible replica of an American swing band!

Conductor, composer, pianist, writer, educator, lecturer, television host, human rights and peace activist, Leonard Bernstein was his own one-person *Gesamtkunstwerk*— Richard Wagner's term to describe the all-embracing synthesis of the arts. Early in his career, Bernstein told the *New York Times*, "I don't want to spend my life, as Toscanini did, studying and restudying the same fifty pieces of music. It would bore me to death. I want to conduct. I want to play the piano. I want to write for Hollywood. I want to keep on trying to be, in the full sense of that wonderful word, a musician. I also want to teach. I want to write books and poetry. And I think I can still do justice to them all."

But perhaps one could subsume all of Bernstein's activities under the rubric of Teacher. "Teaching," he once said in his lecture "A Tribute to Teachers," "is probably the noblest profession in the world—the most unselfish, difficult, and honorable profession. It is also the most unappreciated, underrated, underpaid, and underpraised profession in the world."[4] Over dinner, Bernstein reminded me that the word "education" is related to the Latin *educere*—"to bring forth what is within"—and then added: "Though I can't prove it, deep in my heart I *know* that every person is born with the love of learning. Without exception, every infant studies its toes and fingers, and a child's discovery of his or her voice must be one of the most extraordinary of life's moments."

The grandson and great-grandson of Hasidic rabbis, Bernstein spoke of "this quasi-rabbinic instinct I had for teaching and explaining and verbalizing," for which, he said, "I found a real paradise in the whole electronic world of television." The New York Philharmonic Young People's Concerts, which had begun under the direction of the conductor Ernest Schelling in 1924, was the longest-running series of family concerts in the world. But on January 18, 1958, Leonard Bernstein presented the first-ever televised broadcast of one of these concerts— its subject: "What Does Music Mean?" Over the next fourteen years, he would conduct fifty-three of these concerts that were telecast and viewed in more than forty countries.

During that time, Bernstein received thousands of letters from his appreciative young listeners. Perhaps the most unusual response to one of his concerts came in 1960 when the orchestra was on tour in Denver, Colorado. One afternoon, when Bernstein was taking a walk in a park with Carlos Moseley, the orchestra's assistant general manager, a little boy of four or five marched up to the conductor and hit him. "Lenny was absolutely astonished, as I was too," Moseley later recalled. "And the little boy said, 'You didn't say goodnight to me!' He repeated it until Lenny exclaimed, 'Oh my goodness, the last children's program was the program when we were running overtime and I didn't have time to say my usual farewell.' And this child said, 'You were talking about Mahler!' That this little thing had resented the fact that Lenny hadn't signed off, but had remembered the name Mahler, pleased Lenny and me no end."

Whether teaching children or adults, Bernstein understood that loving and learning are inextricably linked, that real knowledge is a concomitant of the *desire* to know, and that music itself—a meeting of living creator and creative listener—is one of the most efficacious vehicles for teaching. As a conductor, Bernstein experienced the relationship between himself and his orchestra as that of a lover and his beloved. As he remarked at the conclusion of his 1955 *Omnibus* television broadcast "The Art of Conducting":

The conductor must not only make his orchestra play; he must make them *want* to play....It is not so much imposing his will on them like a dictator; it is more like projecting his feelings around him so that they reach the last man in the second violin section. And when this happens—when one hundred men share his feelings, exactly, simultaneously, responding as one to each rise and fall of the music, to each point of arrival and departure, to each little inner pulse—then there is a human identity of feeling that has no equal elsewhere. It is the closest thing I know to love itself.[5]

Bernstein's long-time manager Harry Kraut once provided a heart-stopping little vignette that testified to the indissoluble, rapturous, and profound linkage in Leonard Bernstein's life between music and love. The conductor had just led an impassioned performance of Beethoven's towering *Missa Solemnis* at Tanglewood, and afterward Kraut describes being a passenger in the conductor's car. "He was driving home," Kraut recalled, "and he got more and more excited talking about this boy he had met in San Francisco with whom he was madly in love, and the car went slower and slower until it stopped moving altogether, right in the middle of Route Seven."

SOMETIMES ONE ENCOUNTERS a person who, from the word go, seems always to have been part of one's life.

I first encountered "Lenny" on November 14, 1954—exactly eleven years to the day after his Carnegie Hall debut. I myself was eleven years old, and at five o'clock that Sunday afternoon my mother had turned on the television in our living room to watch a nationally broadcast weekly culture magazine show called *Omnibus*. I'll never forget my first glimpse of the conductor. He was a dark-haired man who was wearing a dark tie and a dark suit—one television critic remarked on Bernstein's striking resemblance to a young Abe Lincoln—and he spoke in a calm, cool, euphonious voice, with the slightest of inflected Boston Brahmin accents, and he was about to *visualize sound on TV*!

On the screen, I saw the first page of the score for Beethoven's Fifth Symphony, blown up and painted white on the black studio floor, and with musicians with their various instruments standing on each stave. The conductor then began to look at Beethoven's rejected sketches for the first movement—with each "rejected" woodwind and brass player walking off the set—and demonstrated with the orchestral instruments how the work would have sounded if Beethoven hadn't disowned them. Then he and the orchestra performed the entire first movement in its final form. The program was a revelation.

Over the next several years, I made sure to watch many of Bernstein's other *Omnibus* programs, such as "The World of Jazz," "The Art of Conducting," and "What Makes Opera Grand?" Then, at the age of fifteen, on my first "real" date with a girl named Beth, we went to see the original 1957 Broadway production of *West Side Story*—truly the *Rite of Spring* of musicals. Though neither Bernstein's electrifying score, nor my vibrant teenage personality, proved to be enough of an enticement to win the heart of my beloved, my musical desires were unfailingly gratified as I assiduously followed Bernstein's career.

Starting in 1958, when Leonard Bernstein became the music director of the New York Philharmonic, I began attending a number of his concerts, both at Carnegie and, later, at Avery Fisher Hall. In those early years of Bernstein's reign, Harold C. Schonberg was the chief music critic for the *New York Times*, as was Paul Henry Lang for the *New York Herald Tribune*, and both of their critical bonnets seemed to have been filled with the same kind of stinging bees when it came to Bernstein's performances. Hardly a week would pass without some disparaging pronouncement—particularly from Harold Schonberg, who wrote venomously about the conductor's "outrageous exhibitionism"... "vulgar performances"..."upstagings" of his soloists... "foot stompings"..."whalings-away" at the keyboard... and, last but not least (heaven forbid!), "overdone ritards." Concluding one of his typical reviews, Schonberg complained: "Bernstein's footwork was magnificent last night. But one did wish that there had been more music and less exhilaration." And reflecting on Bernstein's first season with the New York Philharmonic, he declared: "At all times the aura of show business rather than music-making is present. Thoughtful people are beginning to complain more and more of Bernstein's antics on the podium...and asking if Lenny is ever going to grow up." For his part, Bernstein took the criticism in stride. "I have been hurt and I have been overjoyed by it," he remarked, "and I have been bored by it and I have been incensed, but mostly not embittered. None of this has lasted. It is all ephemeral."

In the years following, I was blessed to attend many extraordinary Bernstein concerts, but there were, in particular, three of them that will never fade from my memory: the now-legendary performance of the Brahms First Piano Concerto with Glenn Gould as soloist on April 6, 1962; the performance of Mahler's *Resurrection* Symphony on December 15, 1971, to commemorate Bernstein's thousandth concert with the New York Philharmonic; and a Carnegie Hall performance of the Beethoven Ninth with the Vienna Philharmonic on November 14, 1979.

It was immediately after the concluding orgasmic apotheosis of the Ninth's final movement that my concert companion turned to me and exclaimed, "Wow! That really was *The Rite of Joy!*" So when she pointed out to me that Carnegie Hall was only a handful of blocks away from Studio 54, she suggested that we walk over to that apotheosis of all discothèques where joy, that "bright spark of divinity," had its all-night sanctuary...though its odes were most likely to be those of Donna Summer's than of Friedrich Schiller's.

In fact, it was Summer's ubiquitous "Love to Love You Baby" that greeted us when we made it through the discothèque's fiercely guarded entrance barrier; and amid the swirling crowd, my friend urged me on to the dance floor. And as we began to dance, we suddenly felt someone bump into us forcefully from behind. As she and I instinctively turned around, we were greeted by a manic wave, a beckoning hand, and the flashing smile of—I promise it's true—the Maestro-Dionysus himself! There he was, wildly dancing—bare-chested under a black leather jacket, a cigarette dangling from his lips—with a retinue of revelers, circling and whirling around him and then around me and my friend as well. It was, in every way, Leonard Bernstein's night of magic and joy.

———————

MY FIRST "LIVE" encounter with Leonard Bernstein was on the dance floor, but my next one would take place under more formal circumstances. In 1988, I asked the editors of *Rolling Stone* magazine if they might be interested in publishing an interview with Bernstein to coincide with his seventieth birthday in August of that year, and they said they would. I then got in touch with his publicist, Margaret Carson, who had years earlier arranged an interview for me with another of her clients, the young conductor Michael Tilson Thomas. Margaret found out from Bernstein's manager, Harry Kraut, that Bernstein was no longer available for interviews, but she decided not to take no for an answer. With a display of generosity I will never forget, she organized a lunch at a Russian restaurant in New York City with

Harry Kraut so that he could interview *me* to ascertain my bona fides and determine whether I might be recommendable to his client. In addition, she also thought it would be helpful to send Bernstein a copy of a book of conversations I had done with the pianist Glenn Gould, who, it turned out, was one of Bernstein's musical heroes, as well as a close and adored friend.

It was a long wait, but at last, in September of 1989, Maggie telephoned to give me the good news that I had passed Harry Kraut's audition, that Bernstein had read my book, and that he had not only agreed to give me an interview but had also suggested that we do so over dinner at his country home in Connecticut on November 20. Overjoyed, I immediately opened my 1989 personal calendar, turned to the page for November 20, noticed that it fell on a Monday, and then wrote down:

DINNER WITH LENNY

DINNER
WITH LENNY

NOVEMBER 20, 1989

LEONARD BERNSTEIN WAS not one for celebrity interviews. "I don't have *favorite* orchestras, *favorite* composers, *favorite* symphonies, *favorite* kinds of food, *favorite* forms of sex," he warned me with a smile when I arrived at his New England country home in Fairfield, Connecticut, on the windy Monday afternoon of November 20, 1989. "So don't ask me those 'favorite' journalist questions."

"I won't, I won't," I promised.

The then seventy-one-year-old white-haired but boyishly ebullient maestro, wearing a sweater and linen slacks, beamed, and led me into the cozy, white-clapboard, ten-room 1750s farmhouse, filled with early American furniture and antiques and bookshelves overflowing with volumes on, as he told me, "every subject under the sun." (I decided not to ask him to name his favorite book.)

"Dinner won't be ready for a couple of hours," Bernstein informed me, "so would you mind if we went over to my music studio and listened to a recording I made about twenty years ago of the Sibelius First Symphony? I'm supposed to perform the work in a few months with the Vienna Philharmonic and I haven't listened to this old performance for years."

So we made our way across the grounds of gingko, mulberry, Japanese maple, and half-weeping cherry trees to the nearby barn-red music studio (formerly a spacious groom's quarters), on whose walls hung scores of drawings, paintings, and photographs, many of them signed. Seeing me eyeing them, Bernstein acted as my docent and gave me a short tour around the studio, and he provided me with a running commentary about those whom he referred to as his "heroes," among them Abraham Lincoln ("That's the famous Mathew Brady portrait of him without a beard"); John and Bobby Kennedy (a portrait taken by Richard Avedon); the legendary French music teacher Nadia Boulanger (pinning the ribbon of *officier* of the Légion d'Honneur on

Bernstein's lapel); and the writer Boris Pasternak (greeting the conductor in his dressing room after a 1959 concert in Moscow where, according to Bernstein's biographer Humphrey Burton, he told the conductor: "You have taken us up to heaven, now we must return to earth. I've never felt so close to the aesthetic truth. When I hear you I know why you were born").

Then Bernstein pointed out to me photos of the film director Luchino Visconti (who directed the acclaimed 1966 Vienna State Opera production of Verdi's *Falstaff* conducted by Bernstein); the baritone Dietrich Fischer-Dieskau (who sang on Bernstein's ravishing recording of Mahler's *Das Lied von der Erde* with the Vienna Philharmonic); the playwright Adolph Green (who co-wrote the lyrics for Bernstein's musicals *On the Town* and *Wonderful Town*); the pianist Glenn Gould, for whom he harbored a special respect and affection ("There he is, my man, my baby!"); and a painting by an unknown artist of the actress Greta Garbo holding a Tarot Card depicting "The Lovers." (In 1945, the producer Hal Wallis of Paramount Pictures seriously discussed the idea of making a "biopic" in which Bernstein would have played Tchaikovsky and Greta Garbo would have played Baroness von Meck, the composer's patroness.)

He next showed me striking drawings of Beethoven and Mendelssohn; a self-portrait of Arnold Schönberg; and photographs of other twentieth-century composers such as Jean Sibelius, Aaron Copland, Marc Blitzstein, Lukas Foss, and one of Igor Stravinsky's grave at the San Michele Cemetery in Venice. (When I brought up the name of Stravinsky's collaborator, Robert Craft, Bernstein exclaimed: "Robert Craft—I could *kill* him—I mean, he spoiled such a lovely relationship between Stravinsky and myself.") There were also photographs of some of his most admired conductors: Serge Koussevitzky ("My great Koussie!"), Bruno Walter, Pierre Monteux, Fritz Reiner ("My great master!"), Arturo Toscanini ("I have lots of Toscanini, he gave me many autographed pictures"), Carlos Kleiber ("What a genius, he's a magician!"), and a blazing-eyed Dmitri Mitropoulos—his predecessor as music director of the New York Philharmonic ("It never *occurred* to me to be a conductor until Mitropoulos one day said to me, *'You must be a conductor!'* ").

Finally, Bernstein concluded the tour by leading me to his most cherished photograph, one that pictured him and his late wife (the Chilean-American actress Felicia Montealegre who died in 1978) seated together at a piano. Then he gently pushed me into a chair next to a table on which lay some Egyptian camel bells that

Bernstein now picked up and shook, as if to signal the imminence of our listening-session, and proffered me a glass of vodka, particularly appropriate for the wintery Finnish music to come.

Dragging, amid fits of coughing, on a cigarette dangling from his lips, Bernstein rummaged through a collection of ancient LPs, dug out a still-pristine copy of the Columbia Records album of the Sibelius First Symphony featuring the New York Philharmonic ("a much-underrated orchestra," the maestro commented), and placed it on a turntable. Softly, a solitary clarinetist began to unwind a seemingly endless sinuous and forlorn melodic line, over which Bernstein, in a tone of mock-grandiloquence, announced: "And did you know that the president of Finland anointed me Commander of the Order of the Lion in 1965?"

Passing his own vodka glass from one hand to the other, Bernstein then started to sing—humming, crooning, moaning, shouting-out gospel-style—as he conducted and danced along to the four movements of the symphony (written in 1898 when the composer was thirty-three). All the while he added recitative-like interpolations, explanations, words of approval and disapproval, and assorted comments for my benefit about this impassioned, mercurial, wildly inventive work.

"Listen, child!" the maestro announced to me. "Here's the Jewish rabbi theme...There's Beethoven...There's Tchaikovsky—it's *Swan Lake*—and just wait for some Borodin and Mussorgsky later on...Some Grieg (but *better* than Grieg)...And now comes Sibelius—just listen, that's *unmistakably* Sibelius. [*L.B. sang and quickly wrote out for me on an old envelope the distinctively Sibelian rhythmic cell we'd just heard:* Dah-*de* dum-dum.] Now, a wind...sighing...And now a pop song [*singing*] 'What-did-we-do-till-we-loved?'...Yeah, that's completely *Carousel*...And now a breeze comes along." Then, as the gorgeous Andante movement came to a close, the now-motionless maestro, glass upraised, bent his head and closed his eyes.

"There sure are a lot of borrowings in there," I said, breaking the spell.

"But it's so marvelous how all music is tied up together!" Bernstein replied enthusiastically, as he went over to the turntable to turn over the record. "I mean, I could go through Stravinsky's *Rite of Spring* with you and point out what comes from Mussorgsky and Ravel— note-for-note passages from Ravel—outright, out-fucking-rageous steals! I could go through Beethoven at his most revolutionary, bar by bar, and show you the derivations from Handel and Haydn and Mozart."

"What about Carl Orff?" I asked. "If you took Stravinsky's *Les Noces* out of *Carmina Burana*, you wouldn't have much left, would you?"

"Orff took nine-tenths of the style from Stravinsky's *Les Noces* and the other tenth from Israeli horas. [*L.B. was now off and away singing and dancing a hora, pounding the table as he went along.*] And Orff was *such* a Nazi. Of course, the Israelis stole from the Romanians. So? It's Stravinsky plus Jewish horas from Romania. Because a composer is the sum total of his listening experience...plus the voice and jism that belong specifically to him: 'I am Wolfgang Amadeus!' 'I am Ludwig!' 'I am Igor Fedorovich!' 'Me, me, Sibelius!' And that makes them instantly identifiable to listeners with sensitive ears. And it's in that sense that I can prove to you in my Talmudic way that Stravinsky's *Le Sacre* is *not* a revolutionary piece and that it *is* a revolutionary piece because there's never been anything like it, before or since."

"Picasso," I said, "once remarked that 'good artists copy and great ones steal.'"

"Right. And part of the artifice of art is knowing how to steal *classy.*"

"But what if it's unconscious?" I asked.

"Of course. It's *all* unconscious."

"There's such a thing as a classy unconscious steal?"

"If you're a good composer," he replied, "you steal good steals."

Bernstein now walked over to the turntable and started to play the symphony's Scherzo and Finale movements. After a few minutes, a particularly passionate string passage ("Jerome Kern would be very proud of this melody") forced from him a sweeping upward right-armed movement and the instruction (to invisible violins): "Now *sing* it on...stand up and *sing*!" Then, a moment later (to me): "Did you catch Jimmy Chambers on horn and Harold Gomberg on oboe? What great guys! They don't make them like *that* anymore."

At that moment, there was a sudden pause in the score. "I have no idea what's coming," Bernstein said, his arms frozen in midair. And then, slowly, as the Finale began gradually to rise to its blazing climax, the symphony all at once stopped dead in its tracks. Lights out.

"What happened to the record?" I asked.

"That's the ending," Bernstein said to me as he lifted the tone arm. "*Dum...Dum.* Two chords. That's it. No diminuendo, no ritard, no nothing...as if to say: 'Fuck you, if you don't like it, go home!' And that's very twentieth century."

"In what way?" I asked, as Bernstein walked over to the couch next to mine and sat down.

"I went to see a Broadway revival of *The Threepenny Opera* the other night," he told me. "A completely misconceived production...but just experiencing that score again, and that Bertolt Brecht libretto, which I've loved all my life!"

"Did you ever conduct it?" I asked.

"I did the world premiere of the Marc Blitzstein version at Brandeis University in 1952—he did the major translation of all time but nobody uses it anymore—with a nine-piece band including a banjo and piano, and with Lotte Lenya playing Jenny. But in this new production— and this is just apropos of Fuck-you endings—John Dexter [the late English theater and opera director] really screwed up because he didn't have a conception."

"Isn't the English rock musician Sting playing the role of Macheath?" I asked.

"Sting is great...or could have been great," Bernstein replied. "That isn't the problem. Frank Rich [the then-chief drama critic for the *New York Times*] reviewed it and got it all wrong—he hated it but for the wrong reasons. What do they know, critics!"

Leonard Bernstein's assistant had earlier prepared and brought down to the music studio a tray of vegetable hors d'oeuvres. And now Bernstein leaned over and passed me a plate.

"Ummm," he said, "what good asparagus, Jonathan, dip it in the hummus. And since dinner isn't ready yet, let me pour you another glass of vodka. You're allowed."

Well, when in Finland, I thought, do as the Finns do—especially when your host is a Finnish Commander of the Order of the Lion. So I let the Commander replenish my glass.

"And now let's press the Rewind Button," Bernstein said.

"The Rewind Button on my tape recorder?"

"No, I mean the Rewind Button in your *head*. I want to do a fast rewind."

"Do you have an Erase Button in your head, too?" I asked him. "That would be extremely useful."

"No, you can try, but it will all come out in your dreams anyway. . . . But anyway, the point of my talking about *The Threepenny Opera* is that so many of those numbers are informed by what Brecht called the *Verfremdungseffekt*—the alienation effect. It's just like the ending of Peachum's song *Das Lied von der Unzulänglichkeit* ["The Song of Insufficiency"]—duh-de-duh *dum-dum*. Done. You don't try to enlist the audience's sympathy, you don't go for a hand, you just do your thing straight out. You say: This is the play, we're actors, this is what we have to say—you pay to watch it, O.K., and if you don't like it, go home. Like the last two chords of Sibelius's First Symphony—there's no ending, no goodnight.

"And in this production John Dexter always tried to go for a hand—the entire production was geared to make the audience *like* them. They ended every song with a strike-a-pose and lights-go-up and now-let's-hear-the-applause. But this goes against the grain of Brecht's and Weill's intent. And then there was poor Sting, who was *born* to sing the role of Macheath, but not surrounded by marvelous opera singers who made him sound like an asshole. In "Cannon Song," Macheath trades lines with Tiger Brown about their days in the army and "Beefsteak Tartare" and all those incredible lyrics [*sings*: Sol-da-ten wohnen / Auf den ka-no-nen/Von Cap bis Cooch-Behar ("Soldiers live/On their cannons/From the Cape to Cooch Behar")].

"Now, all the actors were body-miked, and Tiger Brown was played by Larry Marshall, who's a terrific baritone, so his voice came out *Rrrrr* and, by compari-son, Sting's voice was *nothing*—even *with* a mike. I mean, he's got this rock voice, what are you going to do? He's great, but you don't show him up by surrounding him with all those marvelous singers with their great trained voices."

"So you'd have to choose either one type of singer or the other," I remarked.

"Actually," he replied, "*The Threepenny Opera* should be done by sort of amateurs, like Lotte Lenya, who was the original Polly Peachum and who sang those songs in a semi-professional manner, with no vibrato, and in a Berlin-1920s rough kind of way. It should be done with all the voices like that, or if you want great singing, do it with life-size puppets and a great pre-recorded sound track."

"So how did you go about casting *West Side Story*?" I asked.

"Casting that show was a very tough problem because the actors had to be able to sing *and* dance *and* be taken for teenagers. Hah! Impossible! Everybody said we were crazy and to just forget it. Columbia Records didn't want to invest in it or record it, so Steve Sondheim [who wrote the lyrics] and I auditioned it like crazy, playing the piano four-hands and screaming it out, trying to convey a quintet or all the contrapuntal things, those crazy fugues like the twelve-tone "Cool" fugue. No one, we were told, was going to be able to sing augmented fourths—Ma-reee-*aaaah*—C to F♯. Impossible! Also, they said, it was too rangy for pop music—To*night*, To*night*…it just went all over the place. Besides, who wanted to see a show where the first-act curtain comes down on two dead bodies lying on the stage? *That's Not A Broadway Musical Comedy.*

"So we were very much discouraged. And casting it was the ultimate problem: trying to find teenagers or people who *looked* like teenagers or who, with the aid of a hair piece and some good makeup, could pass for teenagers. So we settled on a mixture—some were actual teenagers, some were twenty-one years old, some were thirty but *looked* sixteen. Some of them were wonderful singers but couldn't dance very well. Or there were great dancers who couldn't sing very well…and if they could do both, they couldn't act. We went through hell.

"And I'll tell you one thing: it saved Columbia Records' ass. Because finally they did record it, reluctantly, under protest—and it kept them from going bankrupt. They had just recorded my *Candide*, which was a flop on Broadway—it ran some two hundred performances and died—though that record eventually became a cult album. But 1957, when *West Side Story* opened, was a very tough year for record companies, which had always depended on their pop sales for solvency. You can't make money releasing the complete recordings of Stravinsky conducted by Stravinsky. So Goddard Lieberson, who was the president of Columbia Records and who was interested in classical music, would balance his losses on classical music with their pop sales in order to do a little Copland or a little Stravinsky. But in 1957 their pop music albums weren't selling. Bebop's appeal was limited and was practically over."

"But Columbia Records had Johnny Mathis," I mentioned.

"Right, that's the thing they could sell. Smarmy pop music."

"Also, Columbia Records didn't get into rock 'n' roll in the late fifties, even though the birth of rock 'n' roll was several years old by then," I mentioned.

"Honey child, there was rock 'n' roll in the late 1930s—before you were born—so don't tell me *that*!" Bernstein exclaimed. "I first heard the phrase rock 'n' roll in a song that Ella Fitzgerald recorded with the jazz drummer Chick Webb and His Orchestra for Decca in 1937—it was called 'Rock It for Me.' It says, opera's out, rock 'n' roll's in. You don't know it? Do you want to hear some of it?"

"You remember it after half a century?" I said disbelievingly.

Undaunted, Bernstein now began to sing, snapping his fingers, growling the horn riffs, and banging on the table in a memorable performance: "So be-*heat* it out in a mi-hi-nor key / Oooh! *Rock* it [*baf!*] *Rock* it [*baf!*]/ Oh, won't you ro-*hock* it for me (WAH!)."

"Wow!" I said. "That's really like an early version of Chuck Berry's 'Roll Over Beethoven.'"

"That was the first time I heard about *satisfyin' my soul with rock 'n' roll*," Bernstein told me, "and I used to go wild when I heard Ella (my angel!) sing that song....So, here am I giving you an education. You can always learn something! [*Looking at his watch*] But we've been talking for more than two hours, Jonathan, and dinner is probably waiting for us. So let's continue the conversation over our meal."

[L.B. and I make our way back to the main house and sit down at the dining room table. As L.B. pours each of us a glass of red wine, his assistant, who has prepared dinner for us, comes in to greet us with two plates of radicchio salad.]

It's so nice of you to have invited me for dinner.

You know, Jonathan, I don't give interviews anymore, I haven't given one in ages. You're a very large exception, and I don't know why. But you caught me on a good day—I'm in very good shape. Maybe because I wrote a little piece this morning for my granddaughter Francisca (known as Frankie). It's called *Dancisca*—to dance to. At the moment it's just one page, but eventually it will turn into something bigger.

And did you know that it's the first piece I've written *all year*, this one-page piece? I've been longing so for this solitude. I just haven't had any solitude until the past couple of weeks, and then only for a few days...in the midst of conducting all-Copland and all-Tchaikovsky programs with the New York Philharmonic, and of preparing for a performance and recording of my *Candide* in London in early December...which is any *minute*. It's the first time that I've actually conducted the work—I've only conducted the overture before—and we'll be recording and filming it. I'm doing it with the London Symphony Orchestra and June Anderson, Christa Ludwig, Nicolai Gedda, Jerry Hadley—and Adolph Green is going to be playing Pangloss. A great bunch.

But when I was brushing my teeth at four o'clock this morning, I heard something like my new little piece—the rhythms first and then the melody—but I got immersed in a crossword puzzle and forgot to write it down. When I woke up, I heard the piece again in the shower, but this time, before going down to breakfast, I wrote almost all of it down, then came over to the studio, finished the piece, and drew the double bar on it just before you got here. It's the first double bar I've done all year!

You once said: "I am a fanatic music lover. I can't live one day without hearing music, playing it, studying it, or thinking about it." When did this obsession begin?

I've always loved music, even as a very young kid. We had one of those big, awkward Atwater Kent radios in the house, and I'd listen to it like crazy—I heard Bing Crosby and Rudy Vallee, but every once in a while there would be a program that featured a whole symphony orchestra. At that time I didn't know what a symphony orchestra was, I didn't even know that there was such a thing as a world of music where you could buy a ticket and go to a concert. And I was fourteen when I attended my first concert, and it was a revelation. It was a Boston Pops benefit for my father's temple—he had to go because he was vice-president of the temple—and it was at that concert that I fell in love with Ravel's *Boléro.*

My father was quite opposed to my being serious about music. It was a very unmusical family, and we never had a piano until one day in 1928 when my Aunt Clara, who was in the process of moving, dumped a sofa on my family—I was ten years old at the time—along with an old upright piano, which, I still remember, had a mandolin pedal (the middle pedal turned the instrument into a kind of wrinkly-sounding mandolin). And I just put my hands on the keyboard—*touched* it—and I was hooked...for life.

So it was just one touch, not just one look.

You *know* what it's like to fall in love. Did you ever fall in love? You're an old guy.

"An old man in love is like a flower in winter." So say the Portuguese.

How old are you?

Forty-six.

A *child*! I'm a quarter of a century older than you. Good God, twenty-five years older!

You were so much older then, you're younger than that now. So says Bob Dylan.

I was ten when I first touched those piano keys...and that was before I could get a hard-on.

I believe that even infants can get a hard-on.

Oh, yes, but I mean getting a hard-on when you *need* one [*laughing*]. And that happened to me at eleven! But at ten I touched the piano, and from that day to this, that's what my life's been about.

I wish I knew what chord you played. But what did you do after you fell in love?

At first, I started teaching myself the piano, and invented my own system of harmony.

I read somewhere that when you were just three or four years old you could already identify pieces of music.

That's just my *mother* saying that, you know. But then I *demanded*, and got, piano lessons once a week—at a buck a lesson—from one of our neighbor's daughters—a Miss Karp. Frieda Karp. I adored her, I was madly in love with her. She taught me beginner's pieces like "The Mountain Belle." And everything went along fine until I began to play—probably very badly—compositions that she couldn't. Miss Karp couldn't keep up with my Chopin *ballades*, so, after a year or so, she told my father that I should be sent to the New England Conservatory of Music. And there I was taught by a Miss Susan Williams, who charged *three* dollars an hour. And now it became a problem, and my father started to complain: "A klezmer you want to be?" To him a klezmer—you know, a klezmer's an itinerant musician in Eastern Europe who, for a meal or a few kopeks thrown at them, played at weddings and bar mitzvahs—was little more than a beggar. And that's what my father knew about musicians.

But then several months later we went to a piano recital by Sergei Rachmaninoff at Symphony Hall—it was the same year that I'd gone to the Boston Pops concert—and my father was just as astonished as I was to see thousands of people buying tickets in droves and *paying* to hear one person play the piano. And it was a revelation—Rachmaninoff was an unbelievable pianist. But still my father balked at three-dollar lessons for me. One dollar for lessons and a quarter-a-week allowance—that's all he allotted for my music. So I started to play in little jazz groups, and we performed at…weddings and bar mitzvahs! [*laughing*] Klezmers! The sax player in our group had access to stock arrangements for "St. Louis Blues," "Deep Night," and lots of Irving Berlin songs…and I'd come home at night with bleeding fingers and two bucks, maybe, which went toward my piano lessons.

DINNER WITH LENNY

Now, my new teacher, Miss Williams, didn't work out very well—she had some kind of system, based on *never* showing your knuckles. Such an incredible idea! I remember her saying, "It's *awkward* showing your knuckles. Camels have humps and they're awkward. So don't be a camel! You have to keep your hands flat at all times." Can you imagine playing a Liszt *Hungarian Rhapsody* like that? So I found another teacher...at *six* dollars an hour...and therefore I had to play *more* jazz. I was *always* at the piano, sometimes at the expense of my homework for school...and it didn't give me much time to play ball with the other kids. And also, when I was fourteen, I started to give piano lessons to the younger neighborhood kids in Roxbury. In fact, my oldest living friend, whose name is Sid Ramin, is somebody I taught piano to in those days. We're exactly the same age, and Sid's an incredibly successful orchestrator, arranger, and composer of the Fiat and Diet Pepsi "Girl Watching" commercials. And he's helped me a lot with the orchestration for works of mine like *West Side Story, A Quiet Place,* and *Mass*—he's the first one I turn to if I need someone to execute and write out my scores if I don't have the time to do so.

A pretty talented bunch of kids you had up there in Boston.

Anywhere you go there are a talented bunch of kids, whether in Omaha or Joplin, Missouri....But meanwhile, I was going to Hebrew school after regular school. I made my Bar Mitzvah speech in Hebrew *and* in English. Leave it to me—I wouldn't make *one* Bar Mitzvah speech, I had to make *two*! And the Conservative temple we belonged to [Congregation Mishkan Tefila] also introduced me to live music. There was an organ, a sweet-voiced cantor—Cantor Glickstein—and a choir led by a fantastic man named Professor Solomon Braslavsky from Vienna, who composed liturgical compositions that were so grand and oratorio-like—very much influenced by Mendelssohn's *Elijah*, Beethoven's *Missa Solemnis*, and even Mahler. And I used to weep just listening to the choir, cantor, and that organ thundering out—it was a big influence on me. In hindsight, I realized many years later that the "gang call"—the way the Jets signal to each other—in *West Side Story* was really like the call of the shofar [*sings: ba-dahhh* dum! *Ba-deee* dum!] that I used to hear blown in temple on Rosh Hashanah.

I think that even Mahler used that shofar sound.

Oh did he ever! Well, we had some things in common in our backgrounds.

I wonder what Mahler's family Passover seders were like when he was growing up in Bohemia.

We always try to have *our* family seders with a minimum of mumbling and a maximum of explanations, and an encouraging of many more than four questions. And then the adults begin to dicker and disagree like rabbis. Sometimes seders result in great dancing and singing, and other times they break out into terrible fights: "Well, that's impossible! That explanation can't be true, the Haggadah's wrong." As they say, a camel is a horse made by a committee—by a *Jewish* committee.

Through your Young People's Concerts, television specials, books, lectures, and pre-concert chats you've been giving people an education for more than forty years. And you once referred to "this old quasi-rabbinical instinct" you had for "teaching and explaining and verbalizing." It's said that in traditional Jewish society, a child, when he was six or seven years old, was carried to the schoolroom for the first time by a rabbi, where he received a clean slate on which the letters of the Hebrew alphabet had been written in honey. Licking off the slate while reciting the name of each letter, the child was in that way made to think of his studies as sweet and desirable.

Societies that have written traditions value them very highly, especially if they're surrounded by hostile people. If you're a Muslim in the middle of a Hindu society, or a Hindu in the middle of a Muslim society, you're forced to do anything you can to pass on your traditions, and whatever they have in the way of written words they coat with honey so that kids will lick them off.

In the Jewish tradition, the one gift that God gave to man in his travail and *tsuris* [aggravating trouble] under the curse of having been expelled from the garden was something called the alphabet. And those twenty-two Hebrew letters are said to have been presented in fire...and that's why those letters, with their strokes and serifs, seem to be like flames. They *burn*. And you can also point to the Pentecostal manner of speaking in tongues with the flames coming down from heaven. So you could say that Christianity is Judaism tidied up a little bit!

Though I can't prove it, deep in my heart I *know* that every person is born with the love of learning. Without exception. Every infant studies its toes and fingers, and a child's discovery of his or her voice must be one of the most extraordinary of life's moments. I've suggested that there must be proto-syllables existing at the beginnings of all languages—like *ma* (or some variant of it), which, in almost every tongue, means *mother—mater, madre, mère, mutter, mat, Ima, shi-ma, mama.* Imagine an infant lying in its cradle, discovering its voice, purring and murmuring MMM to itself...

I have to tell you that I have a new grandchild, my daughter Jamie's son—five weeks old last Saturday...

Congratulations! What's his name?

We call him Spike. His real name is Evan (for his father David's middle name) Samuel (for my father) Thomas. And he looks a little like everybody. Sometimes he's the image of his father, he has his mother's chin, and some people look at him and say he's me!...

So what was I saying?

You were talking about the infant murmuring MMM to itself.

And suddenly it gets hungry and it opens its mouth for the nipple—every kid does it—and out comes MMA-*AA*! ... and it's so good that it learns to associate that syllable with the breast and the pleasure of being fed. *Madre/ mare* (mother/sea) are almost the same word in

Spanish...and in French, *mère/mer* are near-homonyms. The amniotic sea is where you spend your first nine months, swimming in this *mater*—that great ocean in which you don't have to breathe or do anything...it all *comes* to you—even after the trauma of being born, which we never get over.

And why do we go through that?

It's so that shrinks can make money. Otherwise what would they do? You go and lie on the couch and tell them about your birth trauma which you can't remember. But in spite of that, there's still that delight with which children first *learn* to say "MA!"

Then comes the next trauma: one day the kid says "MA!" and the nipple does not arrive. *Oy!* This can happen on day five or month five of the child's life, but whenever it happens, it's an unimaginable shock. Some people go through re-birthing therapy and claim to have relived it. I've never done that one, but I know grown-up guys who have jumped—literally *jumped*—into the arms of their lady therapists and *wept*, hoping to be cradled at their breasts! Great big grown-up fellas with their *shoes* on—well, I guess they have to take their shoes off [*laughing*]—and they come out saying "Wow!" I suppose such a therapist has to be a pretty big breasty lady to receive adults at their bosom.

Maybe if MA doesn't show up, you wind up saying MAH-ler!

[*Laughing*] Why not? It's not a bad joke, it's very relevant.

I've heard that Mahler had to talk to Freud about that problem.

You know, Mahler made four appointments with Sigmund Freud, and three times he broke them because he was so scared to find out why he was impotent. His wife, Alma, who was fucking everybody who was coming by—Gropius, Kokoschka, Werfel, and Bruno Walter, among others—sent him to see Freud. He was twenty years older than she, and she was the prettiest girl in Vienna—rich, cultured, seductive...

Didn't you yourself once meet her?

Certainly. She tried to get me to bed. Many years ago she was staying in the Hotel Pierre in New York—she had attended some of my New York Philharmonic rehearsals—and she invited me for "tea"—which turned out to be "aquavit"—then suggested we go to look at some "memorabilia" of her composer husband in her bedroom.

She must have been quite a bit older than you at that time.

[*Laughing*] She was *generations* older than I. And she had her hair frizzed up and was flirting like mad. (I spent a half hour in the living room, a minute or two less in the bedroom.) She was really like a wonderful Viennese operetta.

As they say, it's not the men in your life, it's the life in your men. And she had some fantastic ones.

She must have been a great turn-on in her youth. But anyway, Mahler didn't pay enough attention to her—she needed a lot of satisfying, and he was busy writing his Sixth Symphony up in his little wood hut all night, and she was tossing around in bed. Mahler was terribly guilty about it all—when he gets to the "Alma" theme in the Scherzo of the Sixth Symphony, the margins of the score are filled with exclamations like "Almschi, Almschi, please don't hate me, I'm dancing with the devil!" [*L.B. sings out the passionate "Alma" theme.*]

Alma's associates had informed her about this brilliant young doctor called Freud whom everyone was talking about and that maybe he could do Mahler some good. But after Mahler had broken his three previous appointments, Freud wrote to him and said, All right, Dr. Mahler, if you don't show up this time, I never want to hear from you again. So when Mahler's steamship docked in Rotterdam on his way back home from America, he finally met up with Freud at the University of Utrecht, where they sat on a campus bench for a couple of hours. And Freud later commented in a letter to one of his pupils, writing something to the effect of: "I have analyzed the musician Mahler"—a two-hour analysis, mind you! Freud was as crazy as his patient—"and I find that he has a Maria Complex. As you will notice," Freud went on, "Mahler's mother was named Maria, all his sisters had Maria for their middle names, and his wife is named Alma Maria Schindler." It was very common in Catholic households to have Maria as a middle name, both women *and* men: Jesús Maria, José Maria, Jean-Marie…

Rainer Maria Rilke.

Rainer Maria Rilke.

[Singing] "I've just kissed a mom named Maria!"

Indeed. Freud thought that Mahler was in love with the Madonna image and was suffering from the Latin-lover dilemma—the mother versus the whore: you worship the former and fuck the latter. Anyway, Freud considered Mahler to have had this problem in spades. Besides, he had a lot of symphonies to write, and very little time in which to write them. It was in the same year that he saw Freud that he died. He didn't even have time to make use of the diagnosis or have a second visit or treatment. He just died. And he didn't die a moment too soon. Believe me, Jonathan, there are no accidents, because he was suffering miserably with what was happening to music, with his brilliant young student and colleague Schönberg, who adored Mahler's music, and Alban Berg, who worshipped Mahler's Ninth Symphony…but they were all moving to destroy tonality, and Mahler couldn't bear it…so he died just in time.

Though didn't Mahler himself wade into atonality's waters?

In his Fourth Symphony he was already fiddling with it—bitonality, atonality, polytonality. The Andante movement of his uncompleted Tenth Symphony almost has a twelve-tone chord—it's eleven tones *at once*. Extraordinary.

But let me press the Rewind Button again. Let's go back to my point about infants who are all born with the *craving* to learn: having experienced the birth trauma, the denial traumas, and the series of other traumas—I almost forgot about gender discovery!—that cause tantrums (the terrible threes, the fearsome fours, the frightful fives), little by little they begin to learn tricks, and they learn to manipulate their parents and aunts and cousins and especially their siblings who start taking all the attention...and suddenly there they are, just in the corner watching. It happens to every child: "I *love* the new baby, Mommy, when are you going to give her back?" It's like that wonderful old Danny Kaye record: "Oh, I love the new baby/I stuck my finger in her ear and she didn't even cry/Maaaaa, are you going to keep that new baby?"

My own granddaughter, according to *her* mother (who is *my* daughter Jamie—the first fruit of my loins, and I'm crazy about her...she plays guitar and piano, and I think she's as good as or better than Laura Nyro), made a great confession when she was two-and-a-half years old. Until then, everything had revolved around her—she was the goddess and queen, and now a new baby was expected: Enter Spike! New baby. *AGHHH!* And apropos of nothing, she would just go into a tantrum—you see, these things just build up unconsciously. Jamie stroked and caressed and calmed her down until she finally admitted: "You know what, Mommy? I don't *like* the new baby." You know from how deep such a confession has to come? And just for her to have come out and *said* that at two-and-a-half will probably save her a good ten years on the couch later on. And so there is this whole series of traumas.

What about when the baby looks in the mirror for the first time and realizes that she's someone else?

Tell me about it!

Mirror-inversion.

[*Laughing*] Yes, mirror-inversion. And then there's *gender discovery*. I'm not trying to give you a lecture on Freud. All I'm trying to say is that each one of these traumas impairs the love of learning with which the infant is born.

You think so?

I know so. And each time a kid learns a new trick of manipulating the sibling or the parent—"I'll scream, I won't pay attention, I won't respond when spoken to"—he or she becomes more cynical, and turns off. They turn off.

Now, if you happen to be born into, let's say, a black, single-parent family in the inner city, even if you didn't have a birth trauma, as well as all those other traumas, you'd be in a lot of trouble. Because you're both impoverished and disadvantaged, *and* you have all those shocks that man is heir to, as Shakespeare said. So if you're not a Hasidic or a Sikh kid who's taught to lick the honey-coated letters—wherever the written tradition is important—by the time you go to school you're already completely resistant to learning. And the bigger the traumas are and the more poverty there is and the more greed there is of the Reagan-Bush kind that we've been living through for ten years, the worse it gets and the greater the attraction of the streets—of crack, or drinking a six-pack and being glued to the television set like a potato ... whatever instant gratification that will take the place of the instant gratification of the nipple.

The nipple is really the original fast food.

Yes, that's the fastest food in the world.

Just to digress for a moment: Everyone who was born after 1945 when that bomb went off is a completely different kind of person from those who were born before then. Because they grew up in a world where the possibility of global destruction was an everyday possibility, to the point where they didn't even think about it that much. But it conditions the way they live.

And if you were my patient in my shrink office, we'd have to begin with that, because *you* exploded with the bomb. You, Jonathan, are already a second generation of the bomb, my baby. And what about people who are half your age, who are twenty-three? It's two entire generations who have grown up with "What the hell, we're all going to die in five minutes or tomorrow or next week." The nuclear establishments are building nuclear arsenals like crazy, and ruining the world as they do it. Unless you have an enemy, there's no way to live. We must have a war economy or we have no economy. And what's wrong right now is that all of a sudden, the enemy has begun to dissolve before our eyes, of its own will... the will of the people: *the Berlin Wall is fucking down!* Do you realize what that means? It's the most exciting single thing that's happened in my lifetime, and I've lived a lot of years. Maybe with the exception of the inauguration of John Kennedy it's the most uplifting and positive historical moment I've ever lived through.

I personally remember living through the amazing days of the anti–Vietnam War movement.

But that was a very bad time. There was nothing positive about that time. We were living under the thumb of Richard-Fucking-Nixon, one of the greatest crooks of all time.

But the point I want to make is that anybody who grows up—as those of my generation did *not*—taking the possibility of the immediate destruction of the planet for granted is going to gravitate all the more toward instant gratification—you *push* the TV button, you *drop* the acid, you *snort* the coke, you *do* the needle. It doesn't matter that it makes you impotent. You've gotten so high and then you pass out in the bed…and you wake up so cynical. The girls wake up unsatisfied, and the boys wake up guilty and ashamed and full of manic fears and anxiety…and guilt breeds fear and anxiety, and anxiety breeds fear, and it goes around— it's that old vicious circle where one thing reinforces the other, which drives you day and night to instant gratification. Anything of a serious nature isn't "instant"—you can't "do" the Sistine Chapel in one hour. And who has time to listen to a Mahler symphony, for God's sake?

I do.

I'm amazed that you do at forty-six. I'm amazed that my children do. My daughter Nina, who's now twenty-seven, has heard Mahler's Second Symphony so often that she knows it better than I do. She's heard it so many times on record and by going to my rehearsals that she knows it the way my sister Shirley knows the lyrics to every pop tune you can mention.

In the sixties, many kids could be seen wearing MAHLER GROOVES *buttons.*

That was nice. That was very nice. I was around then. And I'll bet you didn't know that I made *up* the slogan MAHLER GROOVES. To this day, I've got a MAHLER GROOVES bumper sticker pasted onto the first page of my score of his Sixth Symphony. But you can't say MAHLER GROOVES to kids in Harlem...or, for that matter, to the musicians in the Vienna Philharmonic

Orchestra. Those are *my* kids, but they don't really care about a "groovy" Mahler.

You know, in 1988 I took the orchestra to Israel—think of it: the Vienna Philharmonic!—and one of the works we played in Jerusalem was, in fact, Mahler's Sixth. *That* was an experience! Imagine...this all-Catholic orchestra whose players, before I conducted them, didn't know what a Jew was—musicians growing up in the birthplace of Freud, Schönberg, Wittgenstein, Karl Kraus...not to mention Mahler—a Vienna that had become a city with almost no Jews that was at one time the Jewish center of the world!

Once, when the players were rehearsing my *Kaddish* Symphony for the first time, they stopped the rehearsal of their own accord to ask me what the word *kaddish* meant, and why they were so moved by the piece, and if I could tell them something about it. And I said that we had to finish up at six o'clock because they were also going to be playing at the opera that night, and they had to get across town to the Wiener Staatsoper, grab a goulash and a cup of coffee on the way, and be ready for the downbeat at seven. I pointed this out to them and said that we hadn't read halfway through the symphony yet. And they said, *Wir bleiben*...we'll stay. I polled the whole orchestra and asked them: "How many of you have to play the opera tonight?" Twenty or so hands went up. "What's the opera?" *Ariadne.* Now, Richard Strauss's opera *Ariadne auf Naxos* is no easy job. But *Wir bleiben, Wir bleiben,* they insisted. "Just tell us what *kaddish* means."

So I said that it was related to the word *sanctus,* that what they said in church every week—*sanctus, sanctus, sanctus*—is the same word as *kadosh, kadosh, kadosh.* And they were turning white...and then one of the musicians stood up and said, *Was meinen Sie, Meister? War der Christ Jüdische?* "Are you telling us that Jesus was Jewish?" Like innocent babies! I couldn't believe it. And I got so angry at them and said, "How can you ask me these questions? You've grown up in this city that was the *Judendzentrum* of the world, and you killed them all, or drove them out."

So this went on after other rehearsals, and sometimes even after performances they would grab me and take me for a drink at a bar and continue the conversation. And finally one of the clarinet players explained: "We were brought up from the age of two years old not to ask questions because we would get no answers. So we didn't ask. We picked up a couple of things from magazines and television here and there, but we could never ask."

They didn't know that Jesus was Jewish or that Jesus spoke a language called Aramaic or that in his time he was referred to as Rabbi Yeshua ben Yosef or that *benedictus* meant *Baruch Haba B'Shem Adonai* or that there was a connection between the Old and New Testaments. They were all churchgoing kids, well brought up in the traditions of their Nazi grandfathers. And yet I think of them as my dear children and brothers. People sometimes ask me how I can go to Vienna—Kurt Waldheim is the president of Austria!—and conduct the Vienna Philharmonic. Simply, it's because I love the way they love music. And love does a *lot* of things.

So that's what I was trying to say before about learning and instant gratification. [*L.B. grabs hold of my cassette tape recorder.*] You've got that? You've got that, little machine? You can't "do" the Sistine Chapel instantly—you have to lie on your back and look up at that ceiling and con-template. And we've already lost a whole generation of kids who are blind to anything constructive or beautiful, who are blind to love, love, LOVE—that battered, old, dirty four-letter word that few people understand anymore.

You often talk about faith, hope, belief. Obviously, you're a believer not just in love but also in the idea of continuity.

We must get back to faith and hope and belief—things we're all born with. But unfortunately we're also born thinking we're the center of the universe. And of all traumas, that one is the biggest and most difficult to get rid of. And the hardest principle to absorb is the Copernican one: that you're just another speck on this planet, which is a speck in the solar system, which is a speck in the galaxy, which is a speck in the universe...which is a speck in something even bigger that we don't have the minds to contemplate.

The Kabbalists say that the mysteries of the universe will be revealed to the knowledgeable through seven voices, seven tones.

Yes, I know that. Seven was always a mystical number—seven branches of the menorah...and why do you suppose we have seven days of the week? I just read an article in the *New York Times* the other day about the edge of space, the edge of our universe, which is the edge of time. Time/Space—it's the same thing. It's so spooky that it makes you shiver. We're close, close. And sometimes, especially out here in the country, you can get very close to it, and if you can communicate the sense of this to kids—to anyone—then you're blessed.

DINNER WITH LENNY

The hardest thing in the world is to enter adolescence and have to come to terms with mortality. I once did a Young People's Concert on this theme, in which I talked about Nietzsche, and concluded with a performance of Richard Strauss's *Also Sprach Zarathustra*. No subject is too difficult to talk to the kids about. You just have to know where the pain is, what they're suffering from... and why do they fold their programs into airplanes and shoot them around? Their attention span isn't too great, so you have to anticipate and invent some tricks, in the *writing* and not just in your performance, because you have to anticipate where they're going to start losing you, or when you're going to start losing them—especially the younger ones.

It was Nietzsche who asserted that "in any true person lies a child who wants to play."

And *play* is a very big word. Because we use the word *play* for music—we *play* the piano, we *play* Tchaikovsky's Sixth Symphony. We go to see a Shakespeare *play*. We *play* Macbeth. Hamlet is a *player*. Stravinsky said that music is "the *play* of notes"—twelve little notes... less than half of an alphabet. I'm a compulsive anagrammatist, and I love to do British crossword puzzles for that reason. I take the *Manchester Guardian* every week, I do the weekly one in *The Nation* because it's a British-style puzzle, I do the ones in *The Atlantic* and *Harper's Magazine* because they're very hard. Anagrams are at the heart of these cryptic puzzles where you juggle the letters such that *beard* and *bread* have the same letters but mean completely different things. *Play* technique. And that's all music really is.

My first Young People's Concert—Carnegie Hall 1958—was called "What Does Music Mean?" It was fabulous. And I talked real hard stuff to those kids—no paper airplanes sailed around Carnegie Hall—and they adored it. Not long ago I saw that concert on Kinescope: I came out and bowed, the kids clapped, and I turned around and we played the beginning of the *William Tell Overture*. I stopped after twelve bars and turned around and said, "What's that?" "*The Lone Ranger!*" they all yelled. "Wrong! It's an overture by a guy called Rossini to an opera called *William Tell*. How about that?" "Boooo!" "O.K., I'm sorry that they used it on *The Lone Ranger*, but what's the difference? Music doesn't *mean* William Tell or The Lone Ranger. It's the same exciting piece." "Oooh, I see."

And then we performed parts of Strauss's *Don Quixote* for them without mentioning the name, and I said, "We're going to play you a piece by Richard Strauss, a great guy, and he was particularly good at writing music that told stories and that depicted atmospheres and places. Program music." And I then told them a story I'd completely made up about Superman: "So here's Superman and here's where he's flying through the air," and we played the entire *Don Quixote* flying-through-the-air wind-machine sequence. "Yayyy!" the kids cheered. "Now," I told them, "Superman's got a good friend who's been unjustly imprisoned. He's in jail, he's innocent, and Superman is going to rescue him, right? And because it's nighttime, you can hear all the prisoners snoring," and we played the passage where the sheep are bleating in all different keys and there's a complete racket. And Don Quixote, who thinks it's a great army, rides in on his old nag and lays about him with his sword and scatters all those sheep who go bleating off in all directions. And I said to the kids, "So now Superman's coming into the prison where everyone is snoring, and everyone wakes up as Superman flies into the air." And the kids were thrilled.

At that point, I turned around to them and said, "You know what? I've been *lying* to you the whole time. None of this music has anything to do with Superman. He wasn't even invented when this music was written. It's really about a guy called Don Quixote who's an old knight with his old nag who's gone off into the world to do good deeds." And then we played the ending of the piece that depicts the death of Don Quixote. And the house came down. And the kids didn't feel pissed at me because I'd lied to them—they were thrilled that I told them the truth. And what they knew at the end is that music doesn't have to mean anything except itself. "It doesn't have to be Superman," I told them, "it could just as well be Don Quixote, but it doesn't matter. Just listen to how gorgeous this music is!"

And in another Young People's Concert, I went into such "easy" subjects as "What Is a Mode?" I taught them the seven church modes and twelve Greek modes. I think I got more fan mail for that show than for any of the other ones...because I sang them pop songs in the Mixolydian mode: "Girl, you really got me now/You got me so I can't sleep at night./You really got me/You really got me." Who sang that?

The Kinks.

The Kinks. Right. They adored it. And I sang them a Beatles song in the Dorian mode and another one in the

Aeolian mode. And now those kids will never forget the Mixolydian, Dorian, and Aeolian modes!

In an essay entitled "Children's Conceptions (and Misconceptions) of the Arts," the psychologist Howard Gardner wrote: "We would not expect children to learn to understand computers by having them examine a terminal or a printout. Yet that is the way we expect the young to become sensitive to ballet, theater, and the visual arts. Schools bus them to plays and museums; Leonard Bernstein offers youth concerts on television; and somehow artistic understanding is supposed to result." And Gardner doesn't seem to believe that it will.

But, as I said in the six lectures I gave at Harvard University in 1973 [published in the book *The Unanswered Question*], all kids are born with a language and a musical competence. Otherwise you wouldn't be able to account for a two-year-old child's saying "I like the green ice cream better" in *any* language, whether it's in Swahili or in Dutch. Every child can say it in the language of its parents—"I like the green ice cream better." That's the Pentecostal alphabet I was speaking about before—the letters of fire that God gave us. The *greatest* gift he could give man was the ability to talk and communicate. And a big part of communication is music.

Every kid is born with a sense of rhythm and has the ability to tune in on the overtone series. It's part of the air we breathe, part of our bodies. The harmonic series is in everybody—the octave, the fifth, the fourth, the third, the major and minor seconds. This is provable through physical principles. An infant knows the interval of an octave because his or her mother sings a note or a melody one octave higher than the father does. And every kid knows the fifth, and every kid knows the first two different overtones of the harmonic series. In every country of the world, kids tease each other with the same tune: *nya-nya, nya-nya*—the first two different overtones of the harmonic series. And every child is born with the knowledge of one-two, one-two—he has two hands, two feet, two eyes, he knows two nipples in his mother's breasts, he breathes in and out, he knows up and down, left and right, and he can march: toddle-toddle, toddle-toddle!

A goose toddle!

[*Laughing*] Maybe not quite in rhythm, but he gets it, it's in him. So once we know about one-two, we can also know the exceptions to one-two—we can know about threes. And that's why the triple meter is so sacred and peculiar to us because we are not triple, we are dual. And that's why the waltz is so fascinating, and why young ladies were forbidden to dance the waltz when it first became fashionable.

At its core, what I think you're saying reminds me of a statement made by the Hasidic Rabbi Dov Baer: "Each person consists of a certain song of existence, the one by which our innermost being was created and is defined."

That's beautiful. That's beautiful. And that's a very fancy way of saying what I'm trying to say, which is very simple...though the work to be done is very complicated. Because we destroy our children's songs of existence by giving them inhibitions, teaching them to be cynical, manipulative, and all the rest of it, and this in addition to the usual childhood traumas—as I spoke about them before—which is all part of child abuse and which takes many forms: lack of attention, lack of love.

That's a very dissonant song of existence.

And yet according to your rabbi, every one of those kids has an irreproducible song of existence. And by destroying it we are robbing kids of the natural rights to sing and dance and listen and understand speech and music. Until we realize this, young people are never going to like listening to any kind of music except that which goes with a drum machine and doesn't make any impositions on their time or attention. It's just like masturbating—[*sings*] *"Bay-bee chuk-a-chuk!"* And you have to work on this through teachers and parents, they have to become aware of what they're doing to their kids.

Might all teachers have your gifts!

I love learning, I'm an eternal student, and that's maybe why I'm a pretty good teacher.

You're an amazingly "playful" teacher, but if an adult doesn't have a child within him that wants to play, kids probably aren't going to respond to that person at all.

I don't think that that's the secret, because *everyone* has a child within him. What is that Nietzsche quote again?

"In any true man hides a child who wants to play."

As opposed to a "fake" man? What is a "not true" person?

Well, you talked about the traumas before. And then accompanying them you often find all kinds of phobias and repressions. So that one can become creatively very messed up.

Right, you become hardened, but you can find that playfulness again. We've got to find a way to get music and kids together, as well as to teach *teachers* how to discover their own love of learning. Then the infectious process begins. I have to find a way to make this process come alive *right now* because I'm old—even if playful!—and don't have all the time in the world, so I have to spend it judiciously. Being with young people has kept me alive, I tell you, and I would do *anything* for them. Think of what we can do with all that energy and all that spirit instead of eroding and degrading our planet on which we live, and disgracing ourselves as a race. I will spend my dying breath and my last blood and erg of energy to try to correct this impossible situation....

For some reason, Jonathan, I've just remembered two dreams I had last night that I wrote down, which I haven't done in years—one very beautiful, and the other a guilt dream...but I can cope with it and handle it.

Do you ever talk to anyone about them?

No. "Every maestro his own shrink" is my motto. My business is shrinking *other* people because I've learned about it—not nearly as much as I ought to know, but enough to help a lot of other people. You need love, and that's why I have ten thousand intimate friends [*laughing*] which is unfair to them because I can't give any one of them everything.

The Buddhists say, "Let your heart be like the sun/Shine its light on everyone."

But you know, my dear Jonathan, there is so much inherent goodness in people that if they aren't inhibited by traumas and are given half a chance, it shines through. I had an instance of that recently. I have a new friend, a new lover, and I had to break this news to the predecessor...and it wasn't just as simple as switching lovers because of a whim. And the reaction was so beautiful and so understanding. And when I love somebody, I love them forever...and that makes utter confusion.

By the way: Ute Lemper.

Ute Lemper?

Do you know about this lady?

You mean the German chanteuse?

Yes. I met her backstage in the dressing room after the performance of *The Threepenny Opera* that we spoke about before, and she's gorgeous. I just flipped! Her recent album—it's called *Ute Lemper sings Kurt Weill* with John Mauceri conducting—is sensational. She's *It*...and I think that if I didn't just have a new lover I'd follow her around on her tour!

But here, Jonathan, take one of these whole wheat hot rolls.

I should, but I'm kind of on a diet.

Whose voice do you hear when you say "I should"? Your mother's?

Undoubtedly. How did you know?

I know you.

But it's only my first consultation with you, Dr. Bernstein.

Yes, but I know you. It's all about your imprisoning mother.

Thank you, Dr. Bernstein. Sometimes I get the feeling around here that I really am a patient in your office! And you come highly recommended, but are my fifty minutes up?

[My new psychiatrist was clearly onto something, though it did cross my mind that there might possibly be a little bit of projecting going on. But as a polite guest, I decided to let it pass and not out-shrink the shrink. But then Dr. Bernstein suggested that I tell him some of the things I'd learned about myself during my years in therapy. At which point I mildly resisted his further request that I elaborate on one of the fairly innocuous personal revelations that he'd elicited from me.]

But why not tell me what I asked you about since you've already confided in me about your "shrinkage," for God's sake!

It's you who asked me about that.

No, you started it.

That's not fair, you started it.

Are we having our first quarrel, dear? [*Laughing*]

Are we? [Laughing] But it's all your fault!

Nya-Nya. [*Singing*] "Well, they began it! Well, they began it!"

What's that from?

That's what the Jets and Sharks yell out to each other in *West Side Story*.

Well, I'm sure glad that we've settled that one. But let's come back to the subject of rejecting and being rejected. I wanted to ask you about your refusal last November to accept an arts award from President Bush and to attend a dinner given by John Frohnmayer, the new chairman of the National Endowment for the Arts, in response to his decision to withdraw the agency's sponsorship of an exhibition about AIDS—a result of congressional legislation against government financing of supposed "obscene" and overly political art. At that time you wrote to Bush: "I cannot risk that coming to Washington to be officially honored during your administration might imply that I am an 'official' artist content to collect a medal in kind and gentle silence while hoping for less stifling days ahead."

The last time I went to the White House was during the last days of Jimmy Carter's administration, and I snuck in twenty-one people up the back elevator by conspiring with a security guard! I was being honored at a gala evening at the Kennedy Center [on December 7, 1980] along with Agnes de Mille, James Cagney, Lynn Fontanne, and Leontyne Price, among others—a good bunch. Leontyne and I were the kids—we had to hold up Agnes de Mille, and Jimmy Cagney was in a wheelchair. And the next day my daughter Jamie came home with me to the Dakota, and in the evening we were sitting and just dishing the previous night's happenings—exhausted but

so ecstatic and flying to the heights . . . and then five minutes later we were crawling on the floor. Because the
housekeeper had come running in to tell us that she'd
been in the kitchen when she heard shots coming from
outside, so she ran downstairs and came back and told
us what she'd seen.

[John Lennon, who also lived at the Dakota on the
Upper West Side of Manhattan, had just been shot and
killed shortly before eleven p.m. near the entrance to the
building. It was December 8, 1980.]

*[L.B. and I sit without saying anything for a long
while.]*

I love the White House more than any house in the
world—after all, I'm a musician *and* a citizen of my
country—but since 1980 I haven't gone back there
because it's had such sloppy housekeepers and
caretakers.

With regard to the Jesse Helms–inspired restrictions
on federal funding, the worst thing concerns the removal
of "politics" as an acceptable subject of artistic works.
Because then you'd have to forget Goya, Picasso's
Guernica, Hemingway's *A Farewell to Arms*. Forget
everything. And as for "obscenity": almost the entire

Metropolitan Museum of Art would have to come down—Mars fucking Venus, the whole Rubens collection of gorgeous, large, fleshy ladies with wet thighs, and the naked ephebes from Ancient Greece, Hermes with his cock up six thousand inches....And the picture of *little* Jesse Helms running around the Senate, as if it were the boys' lavatory in a high school, showing dirty pictures to the other senators [*laughing*] is so disgraceful that I cannot ever forgive him.

We had eight lovely, passive, on-our-backs, status quo, don't-make-waves years with Ronald Reagan. The *fights* I had with my mother! "Don't you dare say a word against our president!" she'd say to me. She's now ninety-one years old—God bless her!—and she can't get around that much anymore but she's still very bright and witty. She doesn't like the family name being dragged in the mud...and when she saw my name in the newspaper every day regarding my refusal to attend the White House luncheon awards ceremony given by Bush (or the Frohnmayer dinner), she'd call me up to say, "You're on the front page of the *New York Times*." And I'd say, "Hold your water, baby: I was not only mentioned on the front page of the *Washington Post*, but my *picture* was also on the front page of the *Washington Post*!" And she'd exclaim, "Well, that's *horrible*!" So I informed her that some of my most conservative Midwestern friends—and *not* friends—sent me such congratulatory messages and telegrams and phone calls…people who voted for Reagan ten years ago!

In the past, I've met and argued with the great statesmen of Europe—Helmut Schmidt, Bruno Kreisky, Ted Heath, and François Mitterrand—who always say, "Lenny, why are you so pessimistic and blue and hopeless?" Because I'm always talking about the brainlessness, the mindlessness, the carelessness, and the heedlessness of the Reagans of the world. "Let me have a little more dough so that I can have that *extra* color television set, that *extra* BMW in the garage." But I think there's a turnaround coming, I really do—look at what's happening around the world from Central Europe to South Africa to Haiti. And I'm looking forward to Jesse Helms being routed in the near future.

People like William Buckley, Jr., William Safire, and George Will think of me as "silly Lenny, there he goes again, what does he know, poor soft-hearted asshole musician, talking 'liberal shit' and 'soft talk.'" Sure it's soft…and what's wrong with soft? What's wrong with gentle? Basically, a liberal is a progressive who wants to see the world change and not just remain stuck in the status quo. So, yes, I'm a liberal, but one who believes in people, not in some "thing." And I've never felt more strength and confidence.

What you call "liberal" was once termed "radical chic" by Tom Wolfe in his infamous article/book about the party you gave in 1970 to raise money for the Black Panthers.

Wrong on all counts! It's a legend and it dies hard. It *wasn't* a party, and *I* didn't give it. What happened is that my *wife* hosted a *meeting* in our New York City apartment for the American Civil Liberties Union in connection with its defense of thirteen Black Panthers who, at that time, were imprisoned in the Tombs without access to an attorney or the rights of due process guaranteed in the Constitution. At our reception were one Black Panther to answer for them, a lawyer from the ACLU, and someone from the other side, as well two pregnant Black Panther wives who hadn't been allowed to see their husbands. Felicia offered to have the reception in our apartment in order to raise contributions for the ACLU defense fund and to allow invited friends of ours to ask questions and for things to be debated, and if anybody wanted to participate in the cause, they were free to do so. My wife had requested that the press *not* cover this event. But Charlotte Curtis [the then-Family/Style editor for the *New York Times*] arrived—simply posing as an interested party, we thought—accompanied by a young friend of hers in a white suit. Her escort turned out to be Tom Wolfe. So what am I to do? You can't beat the legends ... except by telling the truth. And ultimately, maybe, legends eventually die. And maybe I can help this one on its way.

[L.B.'s assistant has now returned to the dining room to bring in our main course.]

So help yourself, Jonathan.

Uh oh! I'm afraid to tell you that I'm not sure I can eat that.

It's just a chicken pot pie.

I don't eat poultry or meat.

Baby, it's just a little chicken! [Yiddish accent] *It vouldn't hoit!*

What's that again?

You don't know that story? It really happened in the great days of the Yiddish Theater when the leading actor collapsed onstage during a performance. And a doctor in the audience rushed up to help him, but the actor was already dead. And out of the audience came a woman's voice: *"So gif him a little chicken soup!"* And the doctor stood up and announced that the actor had died...and the woman called back to him: *"Vell, it vouldn't hoit!"* So maybe I can change your life.

I see that Dr. Freud has now turned into Mephistoph-eles: "Faust, how could you have led your life bereft of me?"

But I mean, "What good is a vow if it doesn't get you any-where?" That line...that line...what am I thinking of? *Yes,* it's from Ruth Draper [the twentieth-century American actress who specialized in character-driven monologues] when she's trying to talk to her son Billy's arithmetic teacher: [*L.B. takes on a very* tony *tone-of-voice*]: "He's just *not good* at *mathematics*! And what *good* is it in doing something that doesn't *get* you anywhere?"

[At that moment, L.B.'s assistant returns to the table, and L.B. says to him, "Nobody communicated to you that this man is a vegetarian, did they?" "No, they didn't."

"Well, it's all right, we've got a sort of maniac on our hands anyway!"]

No matter. I may have given up chicken soup for Lent, but I think that music is still the best medicine. Do you know the book Awakenings *by the neurologist Oliver Sacks?*

Yes, but I've only read some excerpts from it in *The New York Review of Books.*

In the book, Sacks describes how he administered the drug L-dopa to patients in a New York hospital ward who had been motionless and frozen for forty years after being stricken by sleeping-sickness...and in one case, a woman he calls Frances D. woke up with terrible jerking and ticcing movements, but when she was exposed to music on the radio or a phonograph, these explosive movements vanished and she began to "conduct" the music and dance—as if the music were able to get her back into right action.

That phrase you used—"right action"—is right out of Zen. That's beautiful.

And Oliver Sacks quotes the German poet Novalis's remark that "every disease is a musical problem, every

Leonard Bernstein, 1947

Photo © Ruth Orkin

Leonard Bernstein, 1947

Photo © Ruth Orkin

Leonard Bernstein, 1947

Photo © Ruth Orkin

Leonard Bernstein, c. 1985

Leonard Bernstein, c. late 1940s

Leonard Bernstein, 1951

Photo © Ruth Orkin

Playing the piano at a rehearsal at Lewisohn Stadium, c. late 1940s

Photo © Ruth Orkin

With Serge Koussevitzky, c. 1948

Photo © Ruth Orkin

With Igor Stravinsky while filming their television program
The Creative Performer, *1960*

Courtesy of the New York Philharmonic Archives

With Glenn Gould, c. 1961

Courtesy of the New York Philharmonic Archives

With Stephen Sondheim, c. 1957

Photo by Robert H. Phillips

*With his wife, Felicia Montealegre, departing for a
tour of Europe and the Near East, 1959*

Courtesy of the New York Philharmonic Archives

Wearing a favorite sweatshirt while rehearsing with the
New York Philharmonic

Courtesy of the New York Philharmonic Archives

Bernstein affixed this bumper sticker to the first page of his score of Mahler's Sixth Symphony

Courtesy of the New York Philharmonic Archives

On the set of the television program Omnibus, *November 14, 1954, lecturing on Beethoven's Fifth Symphony*

Photo by Gordon Parks/Collection/Getty Images

Exiting the National Theater in Washington, D.C., during an out-of-town tryout for West Side Story, *1957*

Photo by Robert H. Phillips

cure a musical solution." What do you think of music's power to heal?

It's a very big field, very big and uninvestigated except by a few people, and I wish I had time to contribute to that one, too, but that's a full-time job.

Do you think that your own conducting might have healing powers?

I could show you hundreds of letters from people who were brought into a concert of mine in a wheelchair and who got up and walked out afterwards on their own.
[A pause]

What composers' works had that effect?

Mozart…Beethoven…Mahler.

I recently played the last movement of your recent recording with the New York Philharmonic of Mahler's Third Symphony to a friend of mine who was extremely depressed at the time…and I have to say there's something extraordinarily numinous and unearthly about your performance of that particular movement, as if one were existing in what the poet Kenneth Rexroth once spoke of as a kind of "lambent aether," where "the air contains something better and more noble than oxygen and nitrogen." And my friend told me that this performance inexplicably lifted her spirits in a profound way. I guess you provided her with a Mahler pill.

Ahhh, that's some pill. . . . But I didn't do it, Mahler did it. The other guys just haven't got the courage to play what Mahler wrote, that's all. I'm a composer, and I understand what he meant. That's the difference.

Pierre Boulez who, like you, is both a composer and a conductor, performs Mahler in a way that is, to say the least, noticeably different from, if not antithetical to, yours. And in his essay "Mahler: Our Contemporary," Boulez, speaking about contemporary performances of Mahler's music, asserts that "the most demanding kind of freedom needs the most severe discipline . . . all the more so because any rash surrender to the frenzy, or indeed the hysteria, of the moment will destroy the original motivation of the music by destroying its essential ambiguity, thus making it hopelessly trivial and emptying it of its

profound content. Furthermore, the latent substructure
is also destroyed and with it the balance between the dif-
ferent moments of the development—and all in the inter-
ests of a chaotic charade by some totally erratic meddler!"
What does he mean by "a chaotic charade by some totally
erratic meddler"?

That's trivial and not to be discussed. Boulez is just intellectualizing. And I think this is a direct attack on me.

I find Boulez's performances of composers like Debussy
and Alban Berg truly extraordinary, but his Mahler
seems not only hyper-Apollonian but too often crusted
over with sheets of ice.

Did you ever hear him do Schumann? You have to leave the hall. [*Sings, in a clodhopping manner, a Schumannesque melody*] De *dah* dah-dah de *dah-dah-dah* / De *dah* dah-dah de *dah-dah-dah*...I mean, forget it. He has no love for it.

I can't believe that an emotional performance necessarily
undermines or is antithetical to the structural aspects of
Mahler's symphonies. That doesn't sound right.

It doesn't. But I have to agree that a *purely* emotional performance, without the inner knowledge of every detail that Mahler has put in—and there are millions of such details—is a hopeless thing, and I've heard performances like that, too. But that implies a lack of knowledge and results in an ignorant performance of the superficial emotions—like being very agitated when the music is agitated.

When he was young, Stravinsky referred to Mahler as Malheur "[misfortune]."

But he changed his mind.

Do you recall the Mahler symphony that you first heard?

The Fourth, conducted by Bruno Walter, when I was in college. And I went to pieces, especially in the third movement.

I've always tried to find the words that would describe the incandescent way you conduct Mahler, and I finally found them in Walt Whitman:

The orchestra whirls me wider than Uranus flies,

*It wrenches such ardors from me I did not know I possess'd
    them,*

*It sails me, I dab with bare feet, they are lick'd by the
    indolent waves,*

I am cut by bitter and angry hail, I lose my breath,

*Steep'd amid honey'd morphine, my windpipe throttled in
    fakes of death,*

At length let up again to feel the puzzle of puzzles,

And that we call Being.

Jesus! I don't remember that, what's that from?

*Whitman's "Song of Myself." He had gone to an opera and
was trying to evoke his experience of that performance.*

That's amazing. Amazing.

*Mahler once made the provocative suggestion that "the
artist represents the feminine element opposing the
genius that fertilizes him"—as if the composer himself
were making love to himself.*

No: as if the composer were *being* made love to by a
divine essence. Mahler meant exactly what Christ

meant. There's the father/son idea, then the eat me/ drink me phenomenon...just as in *Alice in Wonderland*. Alice sees a piece of cake on the shelf as she's going down the rabbit hole, and she eats it and grows taller. Then she discovers a bottle and drinks from it and grows smaller. Eat...this is my body. Drink...this is my blood: *his* body/*his* blood. So he is impregnating his believers. And think of the *Song of Songs*, the sexiest of all poems—"thy two breasts are like two young roes, thy belly is like a heap of wheat set about with lilies, honey and milk are under thy tongue"—in which Christians see Jesus as the Bridegroom and the Church as the Bride of Christ. The Bridegroom cometh. And it all really comes from Eastern religions. Think of the sun god who makes of his worshipers the receivers of his benefits—*his* light, *his* heat—the vessels through which the god speaks. And in a similar manner, the god comes to impregnate Mahler with the divine message, who receives it and writes it down like a good secretary. Just as Mozart did.

And we, as listeners, "receive" his symphonies as if they were musical Rorschach tests—there are so many ways to hear them.

Because the observer has an impact on the thing observed—he or she changes it. So thank God for diversity, for active listeners. If we didn't have *you* listening as opposed to the person next to you, if everybody received exactly the same message, what would be the point? There are far too many passive listeners, including critics, who fall asleep and snore *audibly* during performances. Virgil Thomson [the American composer and music critic] used to snore away.

And then write a review the next day.

And how!

He must have had some interesting dreams.

I remember once when he fell out of his chair into the aisle [*laughing*].

I know you've had your ups and downs with critics regarding your own compositions.

Critics get their rocks off on me, but now I'm at the magic age of seventy, and you can't do wrong after that. But years ago one critic attacked me for being "undiscussable" in the category of new music, saying that I'd opted out. When everybody was writing Boulez and Stockhausen, I was writing the *Chichester Psalms*...and so, fuck me!

And so what.

And so what. Milton Babbitt [the late-American composer noted for his serial and electronic music] once told me that he would have given his left ball if he could have written *Chichester Psalms*...when he had just said to somebody else: "You don't really mean you *like* that music?"

But getting back to all the ways one can hear a piece of music: Haven't you noticed how you can have even varied perceptions in yourself to the same piece heard on different occasions? Listening to, say, Richard Strauss's *Der Rosenkavalier* when you were an adolescent, or as a young man in your twenties making love to a girl while listening to that music? And then hearing it ten years later and having your heart break because you've changed and you know a little more about what the librettist Hugo von Hofmannsthal's words are saying?

In an article you once wrote entitled "Mahler: His Time Has Come," you counterposed a number of dualisms that you thought the composer embodied: Christian/Jew, believer/doubter, Faustian Philosopher/Oriental Mystic, provincial/cosmopolitan, sophisticate/naïf, rough-hewn/ epicene, subtle/blatant, brash/shy, grandiose/self-anni- hilating. And I'm sure it's occurred to people other than myself that many of these dualisms might describe you as well.

Except that I'm not a Christian and Mahler was. He con- verted—like a louse!—just in time to apply for the job of director of the Vienna Court Opera in 1897.

But Arnold Schönberg also converted, though he later reconverted.

But Mahler didn't. And he did it only to get that job. I mean, there were no Nazis pulling out his fingernails then. Whereas Schönberg was fleeing from Hitler.

But Mahler was so obsessed with so many Christian themes—redemption, salvation, resurrection—in his work.

Of course he was…and he also has "Zen" music in it, totally cool Buddhistic music.

It's with a sense of purely skeptical bemusement that I'm asking this... but to me, it feels as if your recent recordings of the Mahler symphonies—even more than your earlier ones—seem like past-life regressions that bring the musical being of Mahler back to uncanny life. And it's often said—and not just by me—that you yourself exhibit such an extraordinary affinity with his musical being that, if I were a believing man—and the truth of reincarnation can neither be proved nor disproved—I think I'd consider you a worthwhile candidate for his being here with us again!

Many psychics have said that. But one even informed me that I was a reincarnation of Wagner! So? Forget it.

In this esoteric vein, Mahler once recounted that on one occasion while he was composing, he heard a "voice in the night" that he took to be that of either Beethoven or Wagner, advising him to "bring the horns in three bars later."

Well, you know how you can introject the voice of Beethoven or Wagner... but, of course, it's your own. You see, your and my friend Glenn Gould wouldn't be here in this room except that he's *in* us. That's why he's here. We *introject* him...and Glenn, and my wife, and other people I love who are dead aren't "up there" walking around and looking like Glenn and Felicia. They don't have earlobes and the same nipples that they had on earth. But somehow they're there, the essence is there. We just don't understand it, our evolution hasn't taken us far enough yet to glimpse what the word that we stupidly use, *soul*, can mean.

I think you're right.

You know I'm right. I don't talk like this to everybody, but I talk like this to you because you know what I know.

Are you suggesting that death is unreal?

Oh, it's *real*, but something goes on—not your name, not your nose, but the *you*-ness goes on. I will swear that Felicia is with me a lot...though not in her shape.

I am frequently visited by a white moth or a white butterfly. Quite amazingly frequently. And I know it's Felicia. I remember that when she died, her coffin was in our living room in East Hampton...and just a few of us were there—the family and a rabbi and a priest, because she'd been brought up in a convent in Chile. We were playing the Mozart *Requiem* on the phonograph. Everyone was absolutely silent. And then this white butterfly flew in from God knows where—it just appeared from under the coffin and flew around, alighting on everybody in the room—on each of the children, on the rabbi, on the priest, on her brother-in-law and two of her sisters, on me...and then it was gone...though there was nothing open. And this has also happened to me here, sitting outside in my garden.... *White.*

[After a long silence, L.B. refills our wine glasses, and his assistant returns to bring us our dessert, which turns out to be two baked pears.]

Have a pear, Mr. Goldstone!

The pears of immortality. And these I "should" and will eat! They look delicious.

And eternal youth is coming up!

You mentioned Glenn Gould just before, and I wanted to ask you about the famous—now infamous—Carnegie Hall concert on April 6, 1962, when Gould per-

formed the Brahms Piano Concerto No. 1 in D Minor
with you and the New York Philharmonic, and when
you spoke to the audience before the performance from
the stage to gently dissociate yourself from Gould's idi-
osyncratic and hyper-ruminative interpretation of the
piece. I was nineteen years old then and fortunate
enough to have attended that Friday afternoon concert,
seated up in the Dress Circle, and I'll always recall it as
being an illuminating, even rapturous musical
experience.

You know what? You're the only guy in the world who can maybe help that legend die, because legends, as I told you before, die very hard. And *that* one about me, Gould, and the Brahms D Minor won't go away.

First of all, the recording of that performance was actually taken from the radio broadcast of the Friday, April 6, concert. But the *first* performance actually took place the previous evening, on April 5, so when those newspaper and magazine articles say, "Bernstein objected to Gould's tempo, but the tempo really wasn't that slow…," well, that's true, it wasn't that slow on Friday. Because Glenn had learned a little something on Thursday night when the performance was almost an hour and a half long!

It was?

It was unbelievable. You have no idea. And I tell you . . . the rehearsals were beyond belief!

What happened was that a couple of weeks before the concert, Glenn called me up from Toronto and said, "Oh boy, Lenny, have I got something for *you!*" And I said, "Glenn, nothing you can do would surprise me. There are no surprises left." And he said, "This time you're going to be surprised. I have the answer to the Brahms D Minor. When can I see you?" And I told him that this would have to happen sometime before the first rehearsal so that I would know what I'd have to do with the orchestra.

So he came over to our New York City apartment, which was in those days just across the street from Carnegie Hall. It was the first time Glenn had met Felicia, and when he arrived, he walked in the door with a fur hat on, and he was wearing a coat and two pairs of gloves and I don't know how many mufflers. So he took off the coat, gloves, and mufflers, and Felicia was very gracious and asked him, "Aren't you going to take your hat off?" And he said, "No, no, no, no, I'll just keep it on." And she said, "Do you *always* keep it on?" And he replied, "Whenever possible!" And then I said to him, "I really have to tell you, Mr. Gould, that I cannot bear seeing you with that hat on. It's so warm in this apartment and you're *sweating*, and God knows but you're rotting your hair under there."

Well, I don't know exactly what happened, but Felicia disappeared with him. Somehow she'd gotten him to take his hat off and had taken him into the bathroom to wash his hair—only Felicia could have gotten away with this—and cleaned it, brushed it, fluffed it up...and twenty minutes later this gorgeous creature, this *angel* with golden hair, now walked back into the room and said, "Ready!"

So he sat down at one of my two little upright Baldwin pianos—set back-to-back—and Felicia and I sat down at the other piano, and he began to play the first piano entrance of the Brahms D Minor. [*L.B. now gets up from the dining table, goes to the nearby piano, and plays that beautiful autumnal passage of "mists and mellow fruitfulness" in a comatose tempo befitting a Japanese Noh drama.*] And so I said to Glenn, "If that's the tempo of your entrance, it means I have to begin the concerto like *this* [*L.B. now plays the menacing, thundering opening of the first movement as if it were an endless drone*], and at that rate it's going to take forty minutes to get through just this one movement!" And Glenn replied [*with L.B.*

now adopting the voice of a demonic Rumplestiltskin]: *"That's exactly what I want!"* "What?" I said. "The orchestra can't play that. The horns don't have enough breath to play even one *phrase* at that tempo." And Glenn just said, "Just wait, you'll see, you'll see."

So I had a rehearsal with the orchestra the next day without the piano, and the musicians said, "Are you crazy? We've played the Brahms D Minor a hundred times, why are we rehearsing it?" And I said, "Yeah, but in this case we have to do it because this is a very special thing—a great guy named Glenn Gould has some rather unusual ideas." So I rehearsed them at Gould's tempo and told them, "I don't want anybody to laugh or protest, we've had sillier things go on here, we do crazy modern music, so just sit back!" And that's how we played it with Glenn at our first rehearsal together.

But the trouble with doing it that way was that we had to play the entire first movement in six instead of in two [*sings methodically: "one-two-three-four-five-six"*]—that's one bar. Then [*sings: "dum-dah"*]—that's two bars. It was just unbearable! And then the second movement was in…guess what? Six! A slow six…so that there was in fact *no slow movement.* And then Glenn played the last movement like this [*L.B. plays the opening passage of that movement in the manner of robotic marching soldiers*]. And there was also always some *mishigas* [craziness] that Glenn had to go through—either because of his chair or his fingerless gloves or his bottled water. So, as I said, it took an hour and a half to get through that rehearsal.

In those days, the Thursday night concert was an open rehearsal, and I would take the audience into my confidence by introducing, say, some aspect of a Debussy piece by talking about Impressionism. And on the night of April 7...what was there to talk about? Well, the performance of the Brahms D Minor Concerto that the audience was about to hear, and I knew that I had to *prepare* them because otherwise we would have had an empty hall at the end of that first movement.

So I said to Glenn, "I always talk to the audience beforehand, what do you think I should say to them? I don't want to talk about the structure of the concerto, or about the idea that Brahms originally meant it to be a symphony, or repeat all those clichés about it being a symphony for piano and orchestra, or a concerto for piano *versus* orchestra, as certain critics of the time had said. So what if we talk about your new revelatory interpretation of the piece?" "A marvelous idea," Glenn responded. "Oh boy, that's really like playing the game!" He loved that sense of the sporting aspect of music—and you remember what I said before about *play* and about *playing* music. And Glenn played *with* it, too. Also, his radio broadcasts were *very* playful, very teasing, *very* scherzando.

Anyhow, he said great, and we concocted the remarks together—I jotted down some notes on the back of an envelope. And I came out onstage and told the audience that they were about to hear an extraordinary performance, that I'd personally never heard anything quite so slow in my life, but I was going along with it because this guy was a very special talent...and let's give it a sporting chance. "Yay!" the audience applauded, so they were "in" on it...and we then played this *extravagantly* slow Brahms D Minor Concerto—it was like an iceberg moving through the Arctic...and nobody left, because they were prepared, and the house came down.

Now, the next performance was Friday afternoon, and I also spoke some words before that concert...and it was this *faster* performance that was taped for the radio. Glenn and I hadn't decided the night before that we should do the concerto a little faster the next day, but he just knew that it had been a little *ungainly* the night before, so I was able to do the first movement in a nice rocking *two* instead of that endless plodding *six*. And we got through it in something like fifty-or-so minutes.

Anyway, the critics went crazy. Harold Schonberg in the *New York Times* accused me of being disloyal to my colleague, though I'd just said that in the case of this performance I was following the soloist faithfully because I had such love and respect for this artist...and, of course, Glenn and I had concocted those introductory remarks *together*. What more can you say? But that's how this legend that I betrayed my *meshugenah* [crazy] colleague began, and this legend has lived on forever.

Glenn was my angel. My wife washed his hair just like Abraham in the Bible washed the angels' feet. Do you know how many times I've sat in this very room listening to Glenn's first recording of his *Goldberg Variations*? During those cold winters when I was writing my opera *A Quiet Place* with my colleague Steve Wadsworth [stage director and writer Stephen Wadsworth] who was sitting exactly where you are now? I remember that one time we were in the middle of a very thorny, impossible second-act problem, and I said to Steve, "Let's listen to the *Goldberg Variations* and clear our heads." And it was like the most beautiful thing I'd ever heard...and one hour later we knew the opera's end.

We were still in the process of working on *A Quiet Place* when Glenn's second recorded version of the *Goldberg Variations* came out just before he died, and we listened to that too—though I still prefer the first recording—and that's when Steve and I created a little shrine for Glenn in this room...and I also put up some pictures of him on the wall.

I sometimes say a little prayer for him when I'm listening to his recordings.

Me, too. I love him...and he's here with us this very *second*, all right?...So now let's have another glass of wine!
   [L.B. fills up both of our glasses.]

At the risk of seeming a bit too lighthearted, I wanted to know if you'd previously heard Vladimir Horowitz's uproarious remark that "there are only three kinds of pianists: Jewish pianists, homosexual pianists, and bad pianists."

[*Laughing*] I'd never heard that one [*laughing again*]. Do you have a question?

Well, Horowitz's little aperçu is certainly belied by Glenn Gould. And moreover, don't you think that today you'd have to expand that Eurocentric list and add to the mix in order to include all those brilliant Asian musicians who are increasingly shining forth?

But there are Jews in Japan and there are homosexuals in Korea! What do you want from my life? [*Laughing*] But, yes, particularly in Japan, the Saito School [the Toho-Gakuen School of Music founded by Hideo Saito], where Seiji Ozawa was a pupil, is largely responsible for that shining forth. And then there are all those incredible violinists who began playing at the age of two months or so [*laughing*]. We don't understand that kind of industriousness... and that's going to continue.

Glenn Gould was always receptive to the latest technological possibilities, and I was wondering what you think of today's widespread use of synthesizers?

In 1988 I let myself be talked into getting the biggest synthesizer you've ever seen. New England Digital sent me its *latest* and *greatest* Synclavier, which had originally been designated for MIT. It took ten days to install it in my studio. Looking like the dashboard of the Concorde—so many blinking buttons you've never seen in your life—it was placed next to my modified piano. A Mac 14-36-B-Jaguar (or something like that) was then brought in, and a printout machine was set up in the adjoining room. All this took *another* week.

Then an "expert" arrived to teach me how to run the Synclavier. They told me that he not only knew about the equipment but that he was a musician. It turned out that, yes, he'd been a jazz musician who'd played some gigs in some motel, but he knew chords and charts. And he said, "You see, it's very simple, it'll just take a day or two." Well, a week later he was still saying "a day or two." And he was followed by a whole other assistant—a young kid with a master's degree from Oberlin who *really* knew all about synthesizers, but he didn't know about this one because *who* could know about this one? And he, *too*, had to be instructed. "Just leave me alone with the expert," he told me, "it's a piece of cake." So they left everything on all the time, and I was told I could improvise to my heart's content all night, and that in the morning they'd come to interpret the printout, which was filled with fifteen tied thirty-second notes in no significant metrical context (and other such notations).

The whole thing turned out to be a wrestling match with the click track (which gives you the bar lines on the printer). Now, *nobody* can beat the click track except with the use of a drum machine…and I *cannot* have a drum machine, I'm just not the type! To prove my contention, I played the slow movement of Beethoven's *Pathétique* Sonata—with no rubato, no *anything*—against the click track. And after *a bar and a half*, we were already not together. Because in the *millisecond* it takes to press the key to produce a singing tone, the printer is showing something that looks more like Charles Ives than Beethoven—an amorphous blob of sixty-fourth notes, two sixteenth notes, and so on. "*You* sit down," I said to my two assistants, "and *you* do it." They couldn't either. Moreover, when I tried to compose, I felt totally inhibited, sitting all alone being watched by that Argus-eyed monster. Finally, after six weeks of torture, I had the system removed, which took *another* week.

So in answer to your question: How do I like synthesizers? Great in the theater pit and on discs. But for composition? Fuck 'em!

How do you like fortepianos [early versions of the piano] and the period instruments that are so popular now in performances of seventeenth-, eighteenth-, even early nineteenth-century music?

Sometimes, sometimes. It depends on the quality of the instrument, and so much on who's doing it.

There are those who say that it doesn't matter who's doing it, and that a bad performance on a fortepiano is better than a good one on a modern piano. That seems pretty perverse.

You're right. I've played Mozart's piano in his Salzburg home, and boy, what a noise it made! Nobody has an idea of that—except for Glenn Gould, who had inklings. And I played Chopin's piano in *his* house in Warsaw... and when I was recently in Bonn I went to Beethoven's house. They had his last piano from Vienna there, completely shattered and untuned and untaken-care-of, but I nevertheless played some Beethoven on it. I know something about the fortepiano, and I also have a double harpsichord in my home—an absolute copy of a Couperin harpsichord from the French Baroque period. And I tell you that if the instrument can bring you closer to the intention of the composer, fine. But you have to have *seykhl* [common sense], too. In my opinion, the conductor Trevor Pinnock's work in this area is particularly exciting—his performances of Bach and Handel make me jump out of my seat!

Do you think it's really possible to listen to (or perform) the century- or two-centuries-old symphonic warhorses of Beethoven, Brahms, and Tchaikovsky as if "for the very first time"—like a virgin, so to speak?

I had that experience with Beethoven's Seventh Symphony when I recently conducted the work with the Vienna Philharmonic in Bonn—the birthplace of Beethoven—at (are you sitting down, are you ready for this?) a Beethoven-slash-Bernstein festival! Dennis Russell Davies presented about ten works of mine with the Beethovenhalle Orchestra, and I was asked, at the last minute, to conduct Beethoven's Seventh—a piece I hadn't done in a couple of decades. So I was still in Vienna and stayed up all night restudying the symphony from bar one, as if I'd never seen it in my life.

"If your mind is empty, it is open to everything," the Zen teacher Shunryu Suzuki once wrote. "In the beginner's mind there are many possibilities; in the expert's mind there are few."

I *am* a beginner . . . all the time.

How do you keep on staying a beginner?

Don't die.

"He not busy being born is busy dying." Bob Dylan said that.

That's a good line. And why do you suppose that Beethoven was always slashing out and crossing out everything? Because he was always beginning, he could always do it better.

It's amazing you say that because in a conversation with the writer Bettina Brentano, Beethoven reportedly said that "although my symphonies always give me a sense of having succeeded, I feel an insatiable hunger to recommence like a child—even though the last work seemed to have been exhausted with the last beat of the kettledrum."

So there!...And in order to prepare for the Bonn concert I stayed up all night making an enormous number of red marks for accents and diminuendi and rebowings in the score. And my poor brilliant assistant conductor, Mark Stringer, had to wait up all night to get all the red marks I'd made. And, as the dawn came up over Vienna, I handed him my corrected score, and he went over to the Philharmonic when it opened and transferred all the marks into all those parts, and then I came and rehearsed the orchestra at eleven.

Now, the Vienna Philharmonic had played the piece a thousand times—at *least*—and here we were, with one rehearsal, flying with it, discovering and creating a really surprising version of this true Surprise Symphony, since that is what the work is all about—shocks and surprises. Because when something is repeated in the score, the accent occurs in exactly the other place from where it appeared the first time—a *left* to the jaw, a *right* hook to the body! And we played it in Bonn twice—the open dress rehearsal filled with all these kids with their scores was almost more exciting than the official performance.

Was that performance in Bonn recorded?

No, and I wish it had been. But how many Beethoven Sevenths can you listen to? I mean, there must be five hundred recorded versions of that piece. Toscanini alone did it three or four times.

And Herbert von Karajan?

Karajan never stopped! Yet another *perfect, shiny* Beethoven Seventh made in the studio. At least my recent recordings are taken from live concerts.

In order to avoid the predictable, boring 501st version?

Well, why else? Not so that you can hear the audience cough. There's nothing like a live event compared to an immaculate studio performance that you put together like a jigsaw puzzle. What I do is to take a live concert and use that as the matrix of a record. Of course we have to do retakes to cover coughs, noises, and wrong notes. But my new albums are basically live performances.

Speaking of von Karajan—didn't he ask you if you would take over the Berlin Philharmonic after he died?

Karajan on his deathbed begged me—three times— "Lenny, they want you, they need you, they love you, you're the only one!"

But with regard to live performances: people are always going to go to concerts, believe me. Laser discs and film aren't going to replace congregating and being together and touching. But the nature of the events will undoubtedly change. You can't remain locked into the tradition of handing down subscription tickets from grandfather to son to grandson—Series B, Series C, Series D. ("Gee, I got Sinopoli, who'd you get?" "Oh, I got Boulez." "Did you get Bernstein?" "No." "Well, I'll exchange my Series X for your Series Y.")

Of course an orchestra should continue to perform Beethoven's Seventh and Tchaikovsky's *Pathétique*: wouldn't it be awful if the "museum" dies? But it will have to change if it *itself* isn't going to fade away. There shouldn't just be the "museum" concerts with the token new piece now and then...or the token twentieth-century masterpiece like Bartok's *Concerto for Orchestra* or Stravinsky's *Symphony of Psalms*. It's just that there should be different kinds of museums for different kinds of stuff. There's got to be a MOMA and a Guggenheim and a Whitney, as well as a Metropolitan Museum of Art. And there have to be other kinds of concertgoing opportunities besides the New York Philharmonic, and I don't mean just going to Alice Tully Hall to hear the Emerson Quartet or the Kronos Quartet. The Philharmonic itself should have quartets and chamber orchestras within it, as well as an associate membership that would include Juilliard graduates who have no place to go—they're first-rate players who still love music, and they can help an orchestra, especially the Philharmonic, because New York City is the music capital of the world.

And the Philharmonic should also have an educational function—the education not only of young musicians who can ultimately replace the members of the old and about-to-retire members of the orchestra, but also the education of different kinds of publics, including kids and old people and people who previously only liked rock music. I'm very sad about the way things are now, but I'm confident that, over time, they'll change.

I've heard that ten or fifteen years ago 60 percent of classical recordings sold throughout the world were sold in the United States, and today it's down to about 30 percent.

Most are sold in Germany and Japan. But don't forget that in Japan all kids receive a Western musical education in the schools. And in this country there are many, but feeble, attempts to bring kids to concerts or operas. Teachers don't have a way of exciting the kids, at the best maybe exposing them once a year to a *La Traviata* or a *Marriage of Figaro.*

And there are fewer and fewer classical music radio stations—"Roll Over Beethoven" is the defining song of the era.

Well, what about television? I did a concert in Warsaw, Poland, this past September—a ninety-minute television show to commemorate the fiftieth anniversary of the outbreak of World War II that was satellited and heard and seen all over the world, including places like Iceland, Portugal, and Australia. But in this country, the prime-time airwaves are per minute and so expensive that even PBS couldn't run it. [At this concert, Krzysztof Penderecki conducted movements from his *Polish Requiem*; Lukas Foss conducted Schönberg's *A Survivor from Warsaw*, narrated by the actress Liv Ullman whose grandfather had died in Dachau; and Bernstein conducted Beethoven's *Leonore* Overture No. 3 and his own *Chichester Psalms.*]

Getting back to our discussion about orchestras, do you think that any of the world's great orchestras are greater or more distinctive-sounding than another?

When a conductor talks about *my* orchestra's "sound," forget it. I have yet to hear a conductor talk about

Haydn's or Ravel's sound. Eugene Ormandy used to refer to "the Philadelphia sound," and he even said something to the effect that, really, there *was* no Philadelphia sound, there was only an "Ormandy sound," and that he could make any orchestra sound like the Philadelphia Orchestra. And he probably could. But what good is that?

Under him, that orchestra advertised its supposed "velvet string sound." But then someone once asked: "Who wants strings to sound like velvet?"

But sometimes you *do* want the strings to sound *exactly* like velvet—in Brahms or Scriabin, say. But who wants that in Haydn or in the Bach B Minor Mass or in the scherzo of a Mahler symphony?

Velvet freaks.

Right... anybody who's queer for velvet. And then they can relax to Gene Ormandy and His Velvet Strings!

So you wouldn't say whether, in your opinion, there's a "greatest" orchestra in the world today?

NO! As I told you when you arrived, I don't have *favorite* orchestras. There *is*, however, such a thing as a particular orchestral tradition and a certain identifiable "sound" resulting from the instruments that musicians have inherited from their grand- or great-grandfathers, as in Vienna... and there is a difference between French and German bassoons and trumpets. There are also "schools" of teaching. But even taking all of these things into consideration, every orchestra can and should be made to sound like the *composer* it's playing, and not like itself—Haydn in Haydn's style, Ravel in Ravel's style, and Mahler in Mahler's style... and not with a "Philadelphia" or a "Berlin Philharmonic" sound. I'm against "sounds." I did a Young People's Concert about that, and it was called "The Sound of an Orchestra."

In your new recorded traversal of Mahler's symphonies, you're using three different orchestras—the New York Philharmonic, the Vienna Philharmonic, and the Amsterdam Concertgebouw. Why?

Because those were the three orchestras that Mahler himself conducted in performances of his symphonies during his lifetime. And they don't sound alike, by any means. But they all sound like *Mahler*—they cry and bite and caress and pray.

You once wrote that "a conductor is automatically a narcissist, like any other performing artist; he is an exhibitionist by profession." But you suggested that there was a difference between the conductor "who is vain on his own behalf" and the conductor "whose ego glories in the reflected radiance of musical creativity."

I've often been said to be an exhibitionist on the podium, but everything I do is *to* the orchestra—what the audience sees from *their* side is their business...I can't be responsible for that. I don't plan any gestures, I've never rehearsed with a mirror. And when my students ask me what they should do to get the orchestra to play a phrase the way I did it, I can't tell them—I have to ask *them* what I did. I can't say: "You put your third finger here and flex your wrist and keep your elbow in." I don't have any recipes or methods. I don't beat time, and I don't allow my students to "beat" music. In fact, I teach them *not* to make a diagonal downward sweep on the third beat the way so-called conducting teachers do—it's like flogging a dead horse. You *make* music. I just advise students to look at the score and make it come alive as if they were

the composer. If you can do that, you're a conductor...
and if you can't, you're not. I've asked members of the
Vienna Philharmonic and the New York Philharmonic,
"How did you follow that, how did you know what I
meant when I was barely moving?" And they'd say, "We
don't know, we just looked at your left eyebrow."

*Apropos of this, Hazrat Inayat Khan, who was both a
musician and a Sufi teacher, once said that "a person
who is conscious of the finer forces of life is able to empty
the capacity he has and make it possible for the life of
another person to reflect upon it. He does it by focusing
his mind upon the life of another, and by that he discovers the past, present, and future. Only he has to put
his camera in the right place."*

And maybe I can put the camera in the right place
because I'm also a composer so that I can identify more
easily with Tchaikovsky or Mahler. Maybe. If I don't
become Brahms or Tchaikovsky or Stravinsky when I'm
conducting their works, then it won't be a great performance. It can be an O.K. performance or a lousy
performance, but the only way I know that I've done a
really good performance is when I'm making the piece
up as I go along...as if I have the feeling that I'm

inventing it for the very first time [*snapping his fin-gers*]: "*Oooh, yeah!* Hey, *that* would be a great idea… let's bring in the English horn here…a bass pizzicato there…now a trombone chord!" And the other way I have of knowing if it was a good performance is not until it's all over, and sometimes it takes me one, two, or even up to three minutes to know where I am or who I am or what's all that noise behind me. Sometimes I've been so far away…so far away.

It sounds like being lost in the middle of the ocean or a desert.

No, it's not *lost* at all. It's *found*…but *away*. And the orchestra is away, too. We're all there. And the longer it takes for me to get back—to turn around and bow—then the more away I know we've been….

I've heard that, starting in 1959, when you were the music director of the New York Philharmonic, you chose some marvelous conducting assistants to work with you. I think Seiji Ozawa was one of them.

He was my first assistant at the Philharmonic. Then Claudio Abbado. And I had three per year after that—Edo de Waart, Herbert Blomstedt among them. And over the years I've taught many young conductors both at the Schleswig-Holstein Music Festival and at Tanglewood.

What do you think are the chances of becoming a successful conductor today? One in a thousand?

I don't know—maybe one in the universe! But I have a few I'd put my hand in the fire for.

Anyone in particular?

Oh, yes. There's a young woman named Marin Alsop. She was a student of mine at Tanglewood—she did Hindemith's *Mathis der Maler* and Roy Harris's Third Symphony under me, and she's fabulous, she is simply wonderful. She's a comer. I have to kick her ass a lot [*laughing*], but I have to kick everybody's asses a lot...

And, Jonathan, I think that I need to have a tea now. Would you prefer tea or coffee?

I'll have a coffee, but it's getting late so I think you should make it decaffeinated.

Should? [*laughing*]

That's my last "should" for tonight.

We'll see.

In one of the six Charles Eliot Norton Lectures that you gave at Harvard University in 1973, you discussed music's basic diatonic laws with regard to the "tonic"—the first main note of a musical key—and the "dominant"—the fifth degree of the scale. And in your comments concerning the first movement of Mozart's G Minor Symphony, you spoke of "the dominant seeking its tonic and each tonic turning into a dominant seeking its tonic, over and over again," as if this movement were a kind of endless loop of continual longing, something that is, to me, conveyed by the German word Sehnsucht, *which suggests the sense of "wanting"...*

Yes, meaning "I need you, I have need of you, because there's an empty place that only you can fill."

And throughout your lectures, I somehow felt that you were, in a way, proposing the notion of music as an art of longing...with tonics and dominants "seeking" and with octaves "reaching."

The opening interval of *Tristan and Isolde* is a rising minor sixth [*sings*], and that's longing, desire. Even Karl Marx spoke of *langsamen schmachten* [to slowly languish]. Intervals that aspire upwards are *aspiring*, and if they go down, they're going *down*.

There's something about up and down, in and out, back and forth. Just listen to the Schubert E-flat Trio [*L.B. goes to the piano and plays an* echt schmachtend *passage from the trio*]. You see what I mean?

So you feel that this is somatically grounded.

Yes, there's an inner geography of the human being that can be captured by music, and not by anything else. That's the real magic of music, that's why Walter Pater said that "all art aspires towards the condition of music"... and that accounts for James Joyce and Gerard Manley Hopkins and Keats and Shakespeare and Hölderlin, or for a diagonal in a Cimabue Madonna—the thing that makes you gasp when you look at the picture. There's something that's echoing an inner geography inside you, and you *feel* it... as in the Schubert Trio, in *Tristan*.

For many years, musical lore has had it that "tonal" music was dispensable—merely culturally and ideo-

logically conditioned. Yet in your Norton Lectures you asked the question: "Whither music?" And among other things, you answered it by pointing to and defending the significant "innateness" of tonality—a system rooted in a preordained and inborn musical grammar known as the harmonic series. It is interesting that almost twenty years later, an increasing number of composers—old and young—are increasingly writing music with obvious tonal implications, or even unabashedly "tonal" music itself. How would you answer your question—"Whither music?"—today?

The return to tonality seems to be coming true. But of course there's no law against *any* kind of music, and there shouldn't be. For a long time, many composers stated that tonality was dead, that serial works were the only thing that could and should be written. Serialism, twelve-tone music, wild chromaticism, neo-classicism, neo-romanticism, Dadaism—all kinds of music can be great, but not to the exclusion of tonality, which, as I said in my lectures, constitutes the roots of music. I think that will *always* be true.

People sometimes take your argument to mean that you simply want to reduce everything to tonality. But somehow I see you trying instead to return, as you suggest, to the rootedness of things.

"The Poetry of Earth." That's the title of the last of my Harvard lectures. John Keats said that "the poetry of earth is ceasing never." And you know what he was talking about? The grasshopper and the cricket. And do you know how his sonnet "On the Grasshopper and Cricket" originated? He and his friend Leigh Hunt, a creditably good poet, were having supper one night and started talking about the grasshopper and the cricket, and they made a bet—not really a bet but rather a game—that after supper they would go into separate rooms for exactly one hour, and each one would write a sonnet about the grasshopper and the cricket. So one hour later each one came out with his sonnet, and they compared them.

Leigh Hunt's sonnet was called "To the Grasshopper and the Cricket," and it's a perfectly lovely sonnet about the cricket, who's a "warm little housekeeper" who "belongs to the hearth," and the grasshopper, who "belongs to the field," and when winter comes, poor thing, it hasn't stored up anything. It's sort of like *La Cigale et La Fourmis* ["The Cicada and the Ant"] by Jean de La Fontaine.

John Keats came out with "On the Grasshopper and Cricket" with its first line "The poetry of earth is never dead." It makes you weep—he was barely twenty-one years old when he wrote that sonnet. He died at twenty-five. And two years before his death in 1821 he wrote [*L.B. recites the following Keats sonnet by heart*]:

Bright star, would I were steadfast as thou art
Not in lone splendour hung aloft the night
And watching, with eternal lids apart,
Like Nature's patient, sleepless Eremite,
The moving waters at their priest-like task
Of pure ablution round earth's human shores,
Or gazing on the new soft-fallen mask
Of snow upon the mountains and the moors
No—yet still steadfast, still unchangeable,
Pillowed upon my fair love's ripening breast,
To feel for ever its soft fall and swell,
Awake for ever in a sweet unrest,
Still, still to hear her tender-taken breath,
And so live ever—or else swoon to death.

Pulsation. Breathing in and out...it contracts and expands, like the universe. And that's what great music does. Each piece in its own way.

In India, the Hindi word "sura" *is the word for both* "sound" *and* "breath."

Yes, and the German word for breath—*Atem*—comes from the Sanskrit word for breath, which is *Atman* [the Self—that which breathes]. Read your *Tristan and Isolde*—the *Weltatem*, the World Breath, as Isolde sings in the *Liebestod*.

Earlier, we were talking about how important you felt it was to get kids interested in classical music. But I now almost take for granted that most kids I meet couldn't care less about it—for them classical music has really gone by the boards. And it's interesting that in 1966 you yourself wrote: "At this moment, God forgive me, I have far more pleasure in following the musical adventures of Simon & Garfunkel or of The Association singing "Along Comes Mary" than I have in most of what is being written now by the whole community of 'avant-garde' composers....Pop music seems to be the only area where there is to be found unabashed vitality, the fun of invention, the feeling of fresh air." And in a wonderful 1967 television special entitled Inside Pop—The Rock Revolution, you wittily deconstructed songs like The Left Banke's "Pretty Ballerina," the Rolling Stones' "Paint It Black,"

*the Monkees' "I'm a Believer," and the Beatles' "Good Day
Sunshine." What do you think of rock music today?*

Boo, hiss! I've become very disappointed with most of
it—*déçu* is the French saying…but it's stronger in
French. *Enttäuscht* in German. In the sixties and
seventies there were many wonderful musicians I liked…
and to me, the Beatles were the best songwriters since
Gershwin. But just the other night I was at a party with
a lot of kids in their twenties, and they didn't know any
of the Beatles songs I happened to mention to them.
[*Sings: "She said I know what it's like to be dead / And
she's making me feel like I've never been born"*].

*Well, one might consider "She Said She Said" one of the
Beatles' more arcane masterpieces.*

All right, but I gave them twelve in a row! [*Sings: "Friday
morning at nine o'clock she is far away / Meeting a man
from the motor trade."*] Did they know "She's Leaving
Home"? Never heard of it. [*Sings: "I don't care too much
for money / Money can't buy me love."*] Never heard of it.
And if I hear one more metallic screech or one more horrible imitation of James Brown, I'm going to scream.
Because any asshole can do it: *"YOU TOO CAN BE A STAR!"*

And you know who's responsible for a lot of this? The record companies! They create terminologies, like "Soft-Acid-Funk-Fusion" or "Blue-Reggae-Rhythm-Blues"—all these hyphenated things...

I have to laugh.

And you'd better laugh, because they're assholes. Every time they create one of these terms, they sell records... and if they don't, they don't. It's horrible, horrible. They just use the kids to make money. Everybody uses the kids. And these kids, who grow up needing instant gratification, know where to go to get it.

And now you see the state you've got me into? Where I'm chewing gum and lighting a cigarette at the same time?

O.K., on to the next!

But I should add that when I was in Spain several years ago, I remember watching huge rings of young people in the square of a Catalonian village joining arms and dancing *sardanas* to a type of band called a *cobla*—dances with twenty-seven counts. I'm a pretty good musician, and the music I could follow, but the dance steps were of such complexity that I couldn't learn them. And talk about innate dance and musical competence! Those people had no idea how complex the dances they were doing were, they just *did* them. It's like those people in Greece who dance to these insanely complicated break-ups of three-eight plus three-four—all those incredible rhythms and tunes that Bartók wrote down in the hills of Greece and Bulgaria. And drunken Greek sailors will come into a *taverna* and start dancing in fives or sevens ... and the band doesn't *know* that it's playing in fives or sevens. *That* is extraordinary music—much more exciting than almost anything the current rock world has to offer, I tell you.

By the way, did you ever hear of a town in northern Spain called Gerona? It's in an amazing part of Catalonia where all those geniuses come from—Picasso, Casals, Miró, and Dalí. Dalí's house and museum are very close by in Figueres. As a matter of fact, I had a date to visit him. His secretary telephoned me to say that Dalí had just come out of a coma and that he had asked to see me. So we made a date for that afternoon, but when I called back to confirm the time, I was told that he had lapsed back into a coma. That was the closest I ever came to meeting him. But I went anyway to the Dalí Museum and spent two days there, and it was an unbelievable experience.

I had gone to Gerona twice—the first time to see and hear the *sardanas* I was telling you about, and the second time was to see the recently excavated twelfth-century town there that had once been a flourishing Jewish community with a synagogue, a cemetery, a *mikveh*—the holy ritual bath house—sewers, houses, and a small astronomical observatory. And this little town's leading light was Rabbi Moshe Ben Nachman, also known as Nahmanides—he was the Chief Rabbi of Catalonia—and his followers would report the position of the stars to him, and he'd meditate and say what it meant. Gerona was the first center of Kabbalistic studies in Spain, and you can't believe the things they turned up there—the tablets and strange inscriptions that have now been deciphered.

Gerona also has an enormous, gorgeous cathedral that was adorned and beautified by the Jews who were good at making gold. There's a gold throne behind the altar which was considered sacred—no one was allowed to sit in it—because it was said that someday not Christ but Charlemagne would come back to sit in it and once again become the head of the Holy Roman Empire. And all the church and business records were kept by the

Jews because they were the only people who could read and write. Gerona is an amazing place, and you should really go to see it.

For years, many rock and many more jazz musicians have been inspired by flamenco music. But over the past couple of decades, a number of rock musicians have also been turning to the East for inspiration, most obviously George Harrison. And in James Joyce's novel Finnegans Wake *you can find the brilliant punning statement: "In that earopean end meets Ind."*

You know, I've always loved Indian music and dance. When I was nineteen or twenty I particularly remember the Uday Shankar Dance Company performing for a week in Boston at Symphony Hall. The beauty of the music and the dancing of Shankar and his lead dancer Simkie (and I remember her name till this day)—with all of its subtle movements of the fingers, hands, and eyes—was unbelievable and completely freaked me out so much that I could barely speak. I could, right now, even sing you the things they did and also play the music on the piano for you—except that the piano won't get the microtones. That music played a big influence in my life, and it had a specific influence on the music that I wrote thereafter, by the way. And I bought all their records—they were RCA Victor 78s—and I knew them all by heart.

And after that first concert, my friend, who knew them, took me backstage where I met the music director Vishnudas Shirali—I remember him like yesterday— and he explained the ragas and then had the musicians demonstrate the sitar and tabla to me. I can't tell you how enraptured I was. And I went back to see them every night—no matter that that was the week of my midyear exams at Harvard, I didn't care if I flunked.

So to reciprocate, I invited Vishnudas Shirali to a Friday afternoon concert at Symphony Hall to hear Serge Koussevitzky conduct Mozart's G Minor Symphony, a different kind of music that I thought he'd enjoy and would be a change for him. But at some point in the first movement, I realized that Shirali was asleep. I poked him and said, "This is the great G Minor Symphony of Mozart." The slow movement began, and he nodded off again. So during the intermission I asked, "What's the matter with you? No reaction at all?" "No," he replied, "no reaction at all. It's baby music—it's for little children. Deh-de-*dah* deh-de-*dah* deh-de *dah-dah*/Dah-de-*deh* dah-de-*deh* dah-de-*deh-deh*. What's that? It's uninteresting." I said: "But what about all those chords? You

DINNER WITH LENNY

137

don't have chords. What about those harmonic changes? What about that crazy sequence in the development section? What about those odd phrases and deletions?" Nothing. I couldn't talk him into it. So I added: "You're just getting even because many Americans fall asleep during those forty-five-minute ragas." The interest there is in the line and in the microtones of the monodic, linear music…and, of course, in the rhythms, which are very complicated, and the drone bass, which never gives up, never gets off that dime. [*L.B. intones a long, deep drone sound.*] And I said, "At least Mozart gets into a subdominant and modulates. Did you ever hear of modulating?" "Yes, that's not interesting, that's for babies," Shirali assured me. "The melodies are so dumb, the rhythms are so ordinary and square."

So I thought: Is it possible that human beings on the same planet, subject to the same laws of the harmonic series and to two-leggedness, etc., can really not talk to each other musically? And I realized that it was just a matter of time, of exposing oneself and being exposed to a new music—like being exposed to a foreign language or foreign customs—and treating it not as the enemy stranger, not as the "alien," but as a friendly cohabitant of the planet. And isn't it wonderful to get to know someone who's a little different from yourself?

And all this took place way back in early 1939. Fifty years ago. It will be fifty-one years this coming January. And I hear it like yesterday. When I think about it, I feel like *then*...I feel like a beginner.

I couldn't help noticing throughout our conversation tonight how remarkable your powers of memory are. This may sound strange, but occasionally when you're talking, I get a sense that your future seems to be returning to your past at the same time as your past seems to be returning to your future, as if you're somehow reversing time.

You can reverse time through memory when memory becomes an anticipation of the event remembered, thereby making it into the future. So that when you remember it, it becomes the now. Think about that.

Proust thought about that, too.

Proust *lived* in that eternal now, remembering the past and turning it into an eternal future, namely, the next sentence he was going to write, the next event he was going to describe, the next character he was going to portray. It's an eternal future for an artist.

Vishnudas Shirali may not have been overly impressed by Mozart, but Mozart, too, was the consummate beginner—and I've always found it interesting that he once stated that he got many of his musical ideas while traveling in a carriage or while strolling after a particularly satisfying meal.

A lot of musicians compose while walking, though I don't. Beethoven, Brahms, and Benjamin Britten composed like that—they heard it and then went home and wrote it down. Someone like Stravinsky, on the other hand, worked from ten o'clock till midday every day...then had lunch, read his mail, had a nap, looked over what he'd done that morning...and in the evening, either went out or thought about how to orchestrate the piece. The next morning—*bam!* Back to composing at the piano. And Copland worked like that too.

It's said that Wagner had to be in a kind of psychotic frenzy in order to compose.

Wagner was *always* in a psychotic frenzy, don't you see, so he was *always* writing music. He was a madman, a megalomaniac.

*What's amazing about Mozart, though, is that he claimed
to be able to hear a complete (or nearly complete) piece in
his mind in one moment! This is what he wrote in one of
his letters: "When and how my ideas come I know not, nor
can I force them. Provided that I am not disturbed, my subject enlarges itself and becomes methodized and defined,
and the whole, though it be long, stands almost complete
and finished in my mind so that I can survey it—like a
fine picture of a beautiful statue—at a glance. Nor do I hear
in my imagination the parts successively, but I hear them,
as it were, all at once. What a delight this is I cannot tell."*

But it's *true*. I've always been on my knees to Mozart. He
didn't mean, however, that he heard the whole piece at
one moment in time. But he could hear, let's say, a bar of
music and see, in his mind's eye, the entire structure of
the piece—he could see exactly where it was all going.
Though don't forget that Mozart was composing at a
time of formulas—sonata formulae, cadential formulae,
rondos, minuets, etc. Just imagine how many times
Mozart wrote [*L.B. sings a characteristic Mozartian
cadence*]. Or the rhythmic figure [*sings: dum dum
ta'dum dum dee-dee-dee*]. Go through the complete
works of Mozart and you'll find it in the *thousands*—
dum dum ta'dum dum. Certain figures, certain motives

are just there. And then he knows that he's going to have to do the second subject in the dominant—he has to decide whether it needs a slow introduction before the allegro, and he knows that, in the reprise, what was in the dominant is going to be in the tonic. Or if it's in the minor key, what was in the relative major is now going to be in the parallel major, or in the tonic minor.

What is *really* to genuflect about is that he could also foresee the developmental structure—in a moment of inspiration he knew what the transition was going to be from theme one to theme two, which cells or parts of the themes were going to be concentrated on and developed in sections or particularly emphasized, and then how he would go about returning to his recapitulation—sneak back to it or crescendo into it or surprise you by bursting out with it. *All* of this is what's amazing. And, remember, I've only been talking now about one movement. In an average symphony or sonata or concerto, we have two or three other movements to think about: which one belongs where, and in what key, and should it be an andante or an adagio, or should there or should there not be a minuet. Whenever Mozart doesn't do a minuet or a rondo at the end, it's an exception. And then there will be another problem that he's set himself, which requires another set of thoughts, another mode of thinking.

Now, I'm not talking about Mozart being able to do this at only some particular moment in his life, because he spent a lot of moments being drunk and fooling around and playing billiards. But somehow he could stop playing billiards, have that moment…and he just *saw* it all in his mind's eye.

In these days I don't think anybody could do that sort of thing because we don't have that prerequisite set of guide rules. Today we can help ourselves to the whole stewpot, including all kinds of serialism, or the wild chromaticisms of Wagner or Scriabin or Mahler, or the neo-classicisms of Bach or Mozart, or the neo-romanticisms of Chopin.

The point is that there shouldn't be any law against any kind of music. In other words, it's the opposite of the time when most composers were saying that tonality was dead and that serial music was the only thing that could be written. Serial music *can* be written, and there's no reason why it shouldn't be. And twelve-tone music is great, and Dadaism is great, and all kinds of music are great, but not at the expense of tonality, which constitutes the roots of music.

What do you think of recent so-called minimalist music?

Yes, it's finding another way to be tonal without being idiotic...but it sometimes *does* come out sounding idiotic; it all depends on the talent of the composer. I mean, Steve Reich is a very talented man, and therefore his music comes out very differently from some of the others of those composers.

And another way that composers are trying to be tonal is through "allusion"—taking quotes from Bach or Beethoven and screwing them up in some foggy way, or dividing the orchestra into two parts where one is playing Scarlatti and the other is playing tone clusters.

I've noticed that there also seems to be a reawakened interest in reevaluating composers such as, say, Boccherini or Jacques Ibert who were once thought of as being a bit mindless.

What you're talking about is *wit*. That's what we have to reinvestigate. And that's what Stravinsky was mainly about in his neo-classic and ragtime periods.

I'm thinking also of Kurt Weill who, in the beginning, was put down by twelve-tone composers such as Schönberg who said that Franz Lehar was much better than Weill was; and then Weill was put down for political reasons; and then, finally, because he went to Broadway. But now one can see his whole oeuvre more clearly.

Again, don't forget his wit. Tremendous wit. That's the Boccherini-Ibert department. And Scarlatti. And Mozart, for God's sake. Wit has always been dismissed as light and therefore not to be taken seriously. In other words, it's not Brahms.

In Wagner's Die Meistersinger, *Hans Sachs sings: "Your closing key is not the same, / This gives the Masters pain. / But Hans Sachs draws a rule from this: / In Spring, it must be so! 'Tis plain!" And regarding these lines, the atonal, twelve-tone composer Arnold Schönberg wrote: "In the development of art, it must always be as it is in spring!" Even though music today lacks that prerequisite set of Mozartian guide rules that you were talking about, you yourself seem to unwaveringly believe in the perpetual springtime-ness of music…an ever-abiding* Rite of Spring!

And how! I feel the meaning of it very deeply….

And O.K., honey child, I just looked at the clock and saw that it's now two-thirty. Two-fucking-thirty! So we've been talking for twelve hours!

[L.B. and I get up from the dining table.]

I know I'm pressing my luck...but just one more question?

You're sure it's just one more?

I promise. And I know you don't like to be asked "what's-my-favorite" questions. But this one time, if you were going to recommend just one of your four-hundred-or-so albums that is most special to you, which one would you choose?

I love my recording of the Shostakovich Seventh with the Chicago Symphony—it's more than a record can be.... But come over here.

[I walk over to the CD player as L.B. holds up a CD.]

This is my personal favorite record that I've ever made in my life, if you'd really like to know.

[L.B. places the disc in the CD player and tells me that we're going to be listening to an orchestral transcription of Beethoven's great C-sharp Minor Quartet, op. 131 that he recorded with the sixty string players of the Vienna Philharmonic in 1977.]

This is so beautiful and extraordinary that I dedicated it to my wife—it's the only record I've ever dedicated to anyone. And I had to fight with the Vienna Philharmonic string players to get them to do it—I actually received personal letters from them saying that it was an impossible undertaking: "Four people can't play that, how can sixty play it?" Well, they can.

I doubled the basses—we had seven of them, and you've never heard basses play so gorgeously—and doubled the cellos judiciously but didn't change a single note or dynamic marking. And finally they loved doing it. You can't understand any Mahler unless you understand this piece, which moves and stabs—and with its floating counterpoint. The orchestra and I performed it at the Odeon of Herodes Atticus in Athens in the open air, and the audience just went out of their skulls. Let me play it for you.

But you must be wiped out.

Never mind. You have to hear a little bit of it ... we'll start midway through the piece with my favorite of all scherzos. Listen!

[Immediately, like a thunder-clap, the éclat of the opening scherzo chord—played at explosively high volume—

literally thrusts me away from the speakers, but as the piece continues, I'm drawn back into the relentless ebb and flow of this oceanic music, as L.B. sings out the quartet's inner voices and occasionally shouts out comments to illuminate some of the structural details for my benefit.]

I've never been able to fathom how Beethoven was able to create this masterpiece when he was totally deaf—but maybe he somehow could hear his deepest self as he composed. And your performance of the music makes me feel as if I've gotten inside Beethoven's brain.

Yes, in his brain…somebody has to be in his brain, that's where we have to be. And you should hear the opening fugue. One more glass of wine, Jonathan, and we'll listen to the fugue…and then it's a night.

But it's in your brain already, and you know it by heart.

I know, but I want to hear it with you. I'm sorry we're playing the piece backwards, but this is *so* incredible that you won't believe what you're hearing. For it is here that Beethoven wrote the impossible. It's not four people fighting with each other, scrapping over a piece of the earth. It's just one endless bow, a love affair. And there was so much love on the stage when we're performing this, everyone in love with everyone else, everyone listening: "Yes, we hear you, we hear you, baby!"

[And L.B. and I listen to the fugue without speaking. When the fugue fades away ("Like a shooting star, a mirage, a flame, a magic trick, a dewdrop, a water bubble, a dream," in the words of the Buddha), L.B. turns to me.]

And *that*, my interlocutorial friend, is The End. Till the next one!

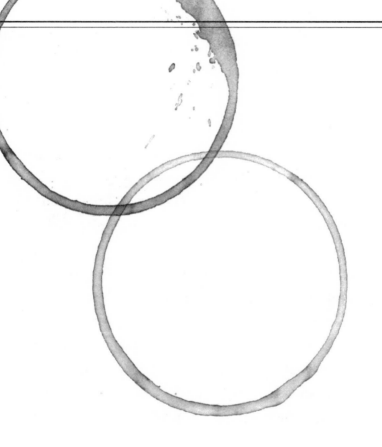

POSTLUDE

AFTER "RECUPERATING" FOR a day following our dinner, I spent most of the next week—tired but elated—listening to the cassette tapes that I had recorded. *Rolling Stone* magazine, which had commissioned me to interview Bernstein in 1989, was allotting a generous eight thousand words for the interview in its pages. What was soon clear to me, however, was that, over the course of our twelve-hour evening, Bernstein and I had spoken more than four times that number. I therefore realized that I would have to transcribe and choose only the major highlights of our conversation to adhere to the magazine's word count. In addition, I also noticed that throughout our discussion there were, as might have been expected, a number of perplexing references, indistinct comments, and unrecognizable names that, for the sake of accuracy, needed to be clarified. So after I had explained my predicament to his publicist, Margaret Carson (who had so assiduously and encouragingly helped to arrange the original interview for me in the first place), she persuaded Bernstein to speak to me on the phone for one additional hour.

I nervously placed the call to him on December 3, 1989, expecting him to respond to me in the way Father William did to his son in *Alice in Wonderland*, one of Bernstein's and his family's favorite books:

"I have answered three questions, and that is enough,"
    Said his father, "don't give yourself airs!
Do you think I can listen all day to such stuff?
    Be off, or I'll kick you downstairs!"

I wasn't off the mark.

"You again!" exclaimed the voice on the other end of the line. "Jesus Christ! You already had me for *twelve consecutive hours...nonstop*! You have enough stuff to write a *book* about me. And maybe you should do it. How many questions do you have for me today?"

POSTLUDE

"I just needed to fact-check a few things to make sure that I'm getting everything correct," I said, trying to mollify him.

"O.K., and if you can also get the typed interview to me in a few days, I'll go over it as well. But I've got to see it right away because I'm leaving for Berlin in three weeks."

"What will you be doing there?"

"Over Christmas, I'm going to be celebrating the fall of the Berlin Wall by conducting two performances of Beethoven's Ninth on both sides of Berlin with an orchestra that will consist of musicians from the Dresden Staatskapelle and the Bavarian Radio Symphony Orchestra, as well as from orchestras from the four countries that technically still rule Berlin—the New York Philharmonic, the London Symphony Orchestra, the Orchestre de Paris, and the Orchestra of the Kirov Theatre, Leningrad. The chorus will be made up of singers from both sides of Germany. And I'll be rewording Friedrich Schiller's text of the 'Ode to Joy' and substituting the word *Freiheit* [freedom] for *Freude* [joy]. Because when the chorus sings *Alle Menschen werden Brüder* [All men will be brothers], it will make more sense with *Freiheit*, won't it?"

"It will. I'd love to be there!" I exclaimed.

"Well, come to Berlin. All my kids are coming if they can."

"Seriously? How do I get in?"

"Knock three times," he replied deadpan, "and ask for Joe!"

Perhaps Joe might have kindly opened the door and taken me under his wing, but I didn't go, and I will always regret having missed those two performances. Fortunately, the Christmas day concert in East Berlin's Schauspielhaus was broadcast live in more than twenty countries to an estimated one hundred million people; and the electrifying recording of that concert, *Ode to Freedom: Bernstein in Berlin*, was released in 1990.

"And by the way," I said to Bernstein, "I know how much you hate these kinds of questions, but a close friend of mine begged me to ask you who were some of your greatest influences."

"O.K.," he replied, groaning, "just tell your friend: Lao-tzu, Moses, Christ, Thomas Mann, Nabokov, Baudelaire, T. S. Eliot, Shakespeare, Rabelais...but mainly my students. But before we hang up," he said to me, "I have to tell you that yesterday I received the most moving telex I've ever seen from the director of the Prague Spring Music Festival. You know, the annual Prague Spring Festival began the year after World War

II, in 1946. And I was there. Czechoslovakia was the first European country I ever saw . . . and then Holland—those two countries with the two unspeakable languages were my introduction to Europe. And I went back for the Prague Spring Festival in 1947 . . . but in 1948 I wasn't invited back because Russia came in, and that was that. And now I just got this telex that says, 'You were here in the beginning, and back then you promised us that when spring would be in all the hearts of our countrymen you would surely return. And that moment has become true.' So I'm returning to Prague in early June to conduct the culminating concert of the festival, with the obligatory program of, guess what? Beethoven's Ninth. This could become a *career* just playing Beethoven's Ninth in newly freed countries. I can't wait to do it in North Korea and China."

Bernstein had graciously answered all my fact-checking questions; and, as he had promised, after I had delivered to him my radically pruned, eight-thousand-word edit of our twelve-hour conversation ten days later, he immediately wrote out his emendations and corrections and returned the manuscript to me with the following note: "Dear JC, I like it lots. I wish there could be more 'you' with more of our 'shrink-talk'; some of our Sibelius-ride at the beginning of our meeting—i.e., more unpredictable things. But it stands as it is, a fine piece. Congrats and affection, LB."

———————

THROUGHOUT OUR DINNER, Leonard Bernstein had rarely been at a loss for a word or a cigarette and would occasionally have to stop speaking in mid-sentence with a racking cough. Throughout his life, he smoked several packs of cigarettes a day, even though, as he brashly told *USA Today* in 1988, "I was diagnosed as having emphysema in my mid-twenties, and to be dead by the age of thirty-five. Then they said I'd be dead by the age of forty-five. And fifty-five. Well, I beat the rap. I smoke. I drink. I stay up all night. I screw around. I'm overcommitted on all fronts." Even the minatory warning in his own *West Side Story* ("When you're a Jet, you're a Jet all the way / From your first cigarette to your last dyin' day") did nothing to deter him from his all-consuming nicotine craving.

Unknown to the public, Bernstein had begun radiation treatments in April 1990 to shrink a malignant tumor known as mesothelioma, which attacks the membrane surrounding the lung. But, undaunted, he managed to fulfill his promise to appear at the Prague

POSTLUDE

Spring Festival in early June to conduct what turned out to be his last Beethoven Ninth.

Just four months earlier—in spite of what was, even then, his noticeably failing health—Bernstein had traveled to Vienna to fulfill another promise. In the mid-1980s, Unitel—a German company that produced audiovisual media—had, in conjunction with Deutsche Grammophon, begun recording and filming Bernstein's second complete cycle of Sibelius's seven symphonies. The conductor had recorded his first Sibelius cycle with the New York Philharmonic in the 1960s—he was the first conductor to have done so. It was, in fact, the vinyl Columbia Records recording of his 1967 performance of the Sibelius First that Bernstein had made me sit down to listen to in his music studio when I first arrived at his home to start our interview, in order—as he had told me at the time—to refresh his memory of the work in preparation for his forthcoming performance of it with the Vienna Philharmonic.

Unitel had previously filmed Bernstein's new versions of the Sibelius Second, Fifth, and Seventh Symphonies; and now, in early February of 1990, the conductor was returning to Vienna to re-record the Sibelius First—with the Third, Fourth, and Sixth Symphonies meant to follow at later dates. Some critics have suggested that the more contemplative, slower-paced recordings Bernstein made with the Vienna Philharmonic during the last ten years of his life somehow attested to a kind of musical burnout—a sign of enervation and a falling-off of his once glittering, jaunty, hyper-energized interpretative powers. In fact, Bernstein's later re-traversals of the symphonies of Sibelius, Tchaikovsky, Brahms, and especially Mahler reveal an incandescent sense of essential mystery, depth, and a hard-won musical wisdom, like the calm *after* a storm.

Viewing the remarkable DVD (brilliantly directed by Humphrey Burton) of Bernstein's re-visioned interpretation of the Sibelius First, one can from the outset observe in the conductor's subdued bearing and countenance a quality of being that the Germans beautifully express with the word *Abendmüdigkeit*—a "gentle evening tiredness." We see Bernstein standing on the podium, momentarily closing his eyes, and then, with an unhurried gesture, signaling with a closed left fist the sinuous and forlorn melodic line of the solitary clarinet that recalls the lonesome sound of the traditional Finnish shepherd's horn.

Suddenly, tremolo strings and stentorian brass awaken the orchestra, setting in motion a work that, in the words of one of Sibelius's early twentieth-century critics, "steps out on new paths, or rather rushes forward like an intoxicated god." And like a born-again Dionysus, Leonard Bernstein, with flickering facial gestures as much as with hands and body, draws forth from the orchestra the mercurial momentum of the symphony, constantly swinging in moods from the impassioned to the melancholy, from the frigid to the candent (and back again). It is a peerless orchestral performance, and the last one he would record, along with Bruckner's Ninth Symphony, with the musicians whom he once called "my children and brothers" and whom he had always urged to embrace his revered John Keats's sense of "a Beauty that must die, / and Joy, whose hand is ever at his lips / Bidding adieu."

———————

SIX MONTHS LATER, a failing Leonard Bernstein traveled from New York City to Tanglewood—the Boston Symphony Orchestra's summer home in Massachusetts—to fulfill his one last desire. It was there in 1940 that Serge Koussevitzky, the then-music director of the Boston Symphony, had chosen the twenty-two-year-old to be one of his first five conducting students. "Koussevitzky taught his pupils simply by inspiring them," Bernstein would say in the lecture entitled "A Tribute to Teachers" that he gave at a Young People's Concert in 1963. "He taught everything through feeling, through instinct and emotion. Even the purely mechanical matter of beating time, of conducting four beats in a bar, became an *emotional* experience instead of a mathematical one. I can still hear his voice now, telling how he wanted me to beat a slow tempo of four beats smoothly, or as musicians say, *legato*. He would say, 'Von-end-two-end-tri-end...it must be vorm, vorm like de sonn!' You see, he couldn't dream of conducting four dead beats, just lying there: one, two, three, four. It was always a question of what happened *between* the beats; how the music moved from one beat to the next...and suddenly the beats came to life. It became an exciting experience just to beat time."

Koussevitzky and his adoring student were later to become close friends—Bernstein loved to quote his famous statement "I vill not stop to rehearse until it vill not be more beautiful"—and the young maestro would never conduct a performance without wearing a treasured pair of cufflinks that Koussevitzky had once given him, ritually kissing them before he walked out onstage. Now, on August 19, 1990, the Boston Symphony Orchestra was going to be playing a concert in the Koussevitzky Music Shed to commemorate the fiftieth anniversary of the founding of the Tanglewood Music Center, and only an occasion of *force majeure* would have prevented him from conducting this memorial concert.

At some point during our dinner that previous November, I had recounted to him a story about the French writer and filmmaker Jean Cocteau who, one morning, decided to return to the block in Paris where he had grown up. Remembering how, as a child, he used to love trailing his finger along the walls of the buildings, he now proceeded to do so again, hoping to summon up a tactile connection to the past. But after an unsuccessful attempt, he suddenly realized that as a child he had been many inches smaller; so now, closing his eyes, he bent down and let his finger trace the wall at this lower height—and as he later wrote: "Just as the needle picks up the melody from the record, I obtained the melody of the past with my hand. I found everything: my cape, the leather of my satchel, the names of my friends and of my teachers, certain expressions I had used, the sound of my grandfather's voice, the smell of his beard, the smell of my sister's dresses and of my mother's gown."

Listening to this story, Bernstein had begun talking to me about Tanglewood and what it meant to him. "That place is very dear to my heart, that is where I grew up and learned so much—and that's where I can touch the wall at the right height. When I go back to Tanglewood I do that thing—I stoop down and touch the wall the way it was in 1940 when I first studied and played there. Just like when I went back to Harvard to give my Norton lectures in 1973 I couldn't keep my hands off those ivied walls. And in fact I was quartered in Eliot House, which is where I lived as an undergraduate."

And now, fifty years later, Bernstein was again standing in front of the Boston Symphony conducting Beethoven's Seventh Symphony, a work he had told me over dinner that he was never finished beginning to understand. But while conducting the third movement Scherzo, he was seized by a coughing fit, started gasping for breath, and suffered a near collapse; but, grabbing the podium rail behind him for support, he somehow managed to recover enough strength to complete the concert by communicating with the orchestra almost solely with his eyes, shoulders, and knees.

Leonard Bernstein had often declared his wish to die on the podium, but that was not to be. On October 9 he announced his retirement from public performance, and heartbreakingly remarked to someone: "I've lost God, you see, and I'm afraid of dying. . . . When you stop loving life, when death's burden takes over, oh there's no point and it's all so useless. Love brings on tears, and I can't cry."

On October 13, a friend came to visit him and, at Bernstein's request, he read out loud Coleman Barks's translations of a number of poems by the thirteenth-century Persian mystic Jelaluddin Rumi, in particular some lines from Rumi's deathbed poem:

Last night in a dream I saw an old man in a garden.
It was all love.
He held out his hand and said, Come toward me.

Leonard Bernstein died at 6:15 the following evening.

His assistant, Craig Urquhart, was asked to choose the clothes in which to bury him. In his biography of the composer, Bernstein's friend and collaborator Humphrey Burton reports that Urquhart "laid out one of the formal dark suits Bernstein wore for the Vienna Philharmonic Sunday morning concerts, with his half-frame conducting glasses and a red silk handkerchief in the top pocket, and Légion d'Honneur commander's insignia in the buttonhole. He chose Bernstein's favorite leather boots. A baton and the score of Mahler's Fifth Symphony were placed in the coffin alongside the body.

In his pocket were a lucky penny and a piece of amber. The children added a copy of *Alice in Wonderland*."

The city of Vienna declared an official period of mourning. In New York City at Lincoln Center—the home of the New York Philharmonic—the flags were flown at half-staff. Broadway's lights were dimmed. His private funeral service, attended only by his close friends and family, took place on the morning of October 16 in his Dakota apartment, where his mahogany coffin stood in state. Afterward, Bernstein's funeral cortège of twenty black stretch limousines made its way slowly through the streets of Manhattan in a police-escorted processional motorcade on its way across the Brooklyn Bridge to the Green-Wood Cemetery, where he is buried next to his wife, Felicia. Along the route, construction workers removed their yellow hard hats, waved, and shouted out, "Goodbye, Lenny!"

POSTLUDE

NOTES

1. Meryle Secrest, *Leonard Bernstein: A Life* (New York: Alfred A. Knopf, 1994), 118.

2. Leonard Bernstein, "Mahler: His Time Has Come," in *Findings* (New York: Simon and Schuster, 1982), 259–67.

3. Barry Seldes, *Leonard Bernstein: The Political Life of an American Musician* (Berkeley: University of California Press, 2009).

4. Leonard Bernstein, "A Tribute to Teachers," in *Findings* (New York: Simon and Schuster, 1982), 180–211.

5. Leonard Bernstein, "The Art of Conducting," in *The Joy of Music* (New York: Simon and Schuster, 1959), 132–63.

SELECTED BIBLIOGRAPHY

BOOKS BY LEONARD BERNSTEIN

Bernstein, Leonard. *Findings*. New York: Simon and Schuster, 1982.

———. *The Infinite Variety of Music*. New York: Simon and Schuster, 1966.

———. *The Joy of Music*. New York: Simon and Schuster, 1959.

———. *Leonard Bernstein's Young People's Concerts*. Jack Gottlieb, ed. New York: Simon and Schuster, 1962. Revised and expanded edition, New York: Anchor Books, 1992.

———. *The Unanswered Question*. Cambridge, Mass.: Harvard University Press/Cambridge Press, 1976.

Bernstein, Burton. *Family Matters: Sam, Jennie, and the Kids.* New York: Summit Books, 1982.

Bernstein, Burton, and Barbara B. Haws. *Leonard Bernstein: American Original.* New York: HarperCollins, 2008.

Burton, Humphrey. *Leonard Bernstein.* New York: Doubleday, 1994.

Gottlieb, Jack, ed. *Bernstein on Broadway.* New York: Amberson, 1981.

———. *Working with Bernstein.* New York: Amadeus Press, 2010.

Gruen, John. *The Private World of Leonard Bernstein.* New York: Ridge Press/Viking Press, 1968.

Hurwitz, David. *Bernstein's Orchestral Music.* New York: Amadeus Press, 2011.

Laird, Paul. *Leonard Bernstein: A Guide to Research.* New York: Routledge, 2002.

Peyser, Joan. *Bernstein: A Biography.* New York: Beech Tree Press, 1987. Revised and updated, New York: Billboard Press, 1998.

Secrest, Meryle. *Leonard Bernstein: A Life.* New York: Alfred A. Knopf, 1994.

Seldes, Barry. *Leonard Bernstein: The Political Life of an American Musician.* Berkeley: University of California Press, 2009.

Sherman, Steve J. *Leonard Bernstein at Work: His Final Years, 1984–1990.* New York: Amadeus Press, 2010.

ACKNOWLEDGMENTS

I am immeasurably indebted and inestimably grateful to the following persons without whom *Dinner with Lenny* would not have been possible: my editor at Oxford University Press, Suzanne Ryan; my literary agent, Sarah Lazin; Marie Carter and Eleonor Sandresky of The Leonard Bernstein Office; and Jann Wenner, who originally commissioned my interview with Leonard Bernstein for *Rolling Stone* magazine.

At Oxford University Press, I would also like to thank the following persons for their invaluable assistance: Joellyn Ausanka, Caelyn Cobb, Patterson Lamb, Jessica Prudhomme, and Isaac Tobin.

For their generosity in enabling me to acquire the photographs for *Dinner with Lenny*, I am grateful to Mary Engel, director of the Ruth Orkin Photo Archive; Richard C. Wandel, associate archivist for the New York Philharmonic; Tom Tierney, director of the Sony Music Archives Library; Toby Silver of Sony Music;

and Ian P. Phillips, who provided me with two photographs taken by his father, Robert H. Phillips.

My deepest thanks go to Annie Druyan, Elizabeth Garnsey, and Richard Gere for their continuous encouragement and support.

INDEX

INDEX

INDEX

INDEX

176

INDEX

177

INDEX

INDEX

music
as art of longing, 126–27
Asian performers, 109
classical music sales, 118–19
as communication, 73
diatonic laws, 126
harmonic series, 128, 138
healing power of, 88–89
impact of listeners on, 94–95
minimalist music, 143–44
Mozart's era, 141–43
rock 'n' roll, 131–33
serialism, 143
tonality, 127–29, 143
wit in, 144–45
Mussorgsky, Modest, 33

Nabokov, Vladimir, 155
Nahmanides (Rabbi Moshe Ben
Nachman), 135
narcissism, 122
The Nation, 69
National Endowment for the Arts, 81
Nazis, 66, 97
neo-classicism, 128, 143
neo-romanticism, 128
New England Conservatory of
Music, 47
New England Digital, 109
New York City, 165
New York Herald Tribune, 21–22
New York Philharmonic
Berlin Wall concerts, 154
Bernstein as director, 13, 21–23, 124
educational function of, 118
Mahler symphonies, 121
Mitropoulos as director, 31
Piano Concerto No.1 in D Minor
(Brahms), 100–107
The Rite of Spring, 6
Rodzinski as director, 7
Sibelius symphonies, 158
Third Symphony (Mahler), 89–90
Young People's Concerts, 17
See also photo section

The New York Review of Books, 88
New York Times
Bernstein interview, 16
Bernstein rejects White House
invitation, 83
Black Panthers, 86
reviews of Bernstein, 21–22
Rich as critic, 36
Nietzsche, 68, 75–76
Ninth Symphony (Beethoven), 154,
156–58
Ninth Symphony
(Bruckner), 160
Ninth Symphony (Mahler), 57
Nixon, Richard, 14, 62
Novalis, 88–89
nuclear weapons, 61
Nyro, Laura, 58

Oberlin College, 110
obscenity, 82–83
Odeon of Herodes Atticus, 147
Ode to Freedom: Bernstein in Berlin, 155
"Ode to Joy," 10–11, 154
Omnibus (television), 18–21. *See also*
photo section
Onassis, Jacqueline Kennedy, 14
"On the Grasshopper and Cricket,"
129–30
On the Town, 15, 30
On the Waterfront, 15
Orchestra of the Kirov Theatre, 154
orchestras, sound of, 119–21
Orchestre de Paris, 154
Orff, Carl, 34
Ormandy, Eugene, 120
overtone series, 73
Ozawa, Seiji, 109, 124

"Paint It Black," 131
Paramount Pictures, 30
Paris, 162
Pasternak, Boris, 30
Pater, Walter, 127
Pathétique Sonata, 111, 117

INDEX